TWO BROTHERS

TWO BROTHERS

A FABLE ON FILM AND HOW IT WAS TOLD

by JEAN-JACQUES ANNAUD

Edited by DIANA LANDAU

Designed by TIMOTHY SHANER

A NEWMARKET PICTORIAL MOVIEBOOK

NEWMARKET PRESS · NEW YORK

This book is published in the United States of America.

FIRST EDITION

10 9 8 7 6 5 4 3 2 1

Library of Congress Cataloging-in-Publication Data available upon request.

ISBN 1-55704-631-X (paperback)   ISBN 1-55704-630-1 (hardcover)

QUANTITY PURCHASES
Companies, professional groups, clubs, and other organizations may qualify for special terms when ordering quantities of this title. For information, write Special Sales Department, Newmarket Press, 18 East 48th Street, New York, NY 10017; call (212) 832-3575; fax (212) 832-3629; or e-mail mailbox@newmarketpress.com.

www.newmarketpress.com

Design by Timothy Shaner
Contributing writer: Amanda Brand

Manufactured in the United States of America.

OTHER NEWMARKET PICTORIAL MOVIEBOOKS INCLUDE:

Van Helsing: The Making of the Legend
The Alamo: The Illustrated Story of the Epic Film
Cold Mountain: The Journey from Book to Film
In America: A Portrait of the Film
The Hulk: The Illustrated Screenplay
The Art of X2: The Collector's Edition
The Art of X2: The Making of the Blockbuster Film
Gods and Generals: The Illustrated Story of the Epic Civil War Film
Chicago: From Stage to Screen—The Movie and Illustrated Lyrics
Frida: Bringing Frida Kahlo's Life and Art to Film
E.T.: The Extra-Terrestrial
Moulin Rouge: The Splendid Book That Charts the Journey of Baz Luhrmann's Motion Picture
The Art of The Matrix
Crouching Tiger, Hidden Dragon: A Portrait of the Ang Lee Film
Gladiator: The Making of the Ridley Scott Epic

Contents

Through the Eye of the Tiger

How Two Brothers Came to the Screen

The Three Passions of Jean-Jacques Annaud

Once upon a time in France... there lived a boy with a boundless appetite for stories, a quirky fondness for old religious buildings—the older the better—an affinity for cameras, and an unshakable belief that "everything is possible." His suburban parents read to him from the animal fables of LaFontaine and the adventures of the great traveler Babar. They took him to the movies every Sunday. They bought him his first Brownie camera at age eight, with which he promptly started taking pictures of every crumbling medieval church and monastery in the surrounding area or spotted on their vacation travels.

At about the same age he received a subscription to *Mickey Mouse* magazine, which brought not only cartoons of the famous Disney characters but a comic strip featuring a saga of prehistoric times called *Quest for Fire*, which he devoured. He also discovered his mother's camera catalog and recognized that movie cameras were the magical machines that transported him into other worlds on Sunday afternoons. At eleven, he acquired his own Super 8 movie camera, with which he produced his first film: "A Documentary on Romanesque Frescoes in Saint-Savin-sur-Gardetempe."

So it surprised no one that this boy chose to pursue his higher education in filmmaking. After graduating first in his class from the Vaugirard School in Paris, specializing in the technical aspects of film, he entered IDHEC (the Higher Institute of Cinematographic Studies), graduating at just age twenty.

And over the next forty years, Jean-Jacques Annaud created a brilliant if highly unconventional career as a film director, first in advertising and then in feature films. A career that took off quickly with a surprise Oscar for his first feature, *Black and White in Color*. Brought an epic struggle to make a movie about prehistoric humans, inspired by his old favorite comic strip, which became the international hit *Quest for Fire*. Led him to adapt a classic adventure tale about animals in the great North (*The Bear*), an esoteric medieval mystery novel set in a monastery (*The Name of the Rose*), a true-life travel odyssey (*Seven Years in Tibet*), and an urban legend from World War II (*Enemy at the Gates*).

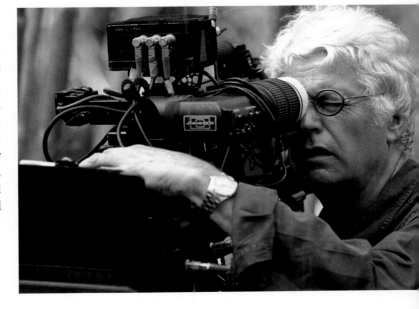

Jean-Jacques Annaud checks a shot with the high-definition video camera used extensively in shooting Two Brothers.

Living with Animals

Jean-Jacques Annaud has felt an attachment to the animal kingdom since bonding with his childhood dog, Flicka, "the one person I could talk to." An only child who was often on his own, he spent lots of time roaming the suburbs on his bicycle, watching birds, collecting butterflies, peering at insects through a magnifying glass. "The animal world was reassuring, a way to understand myself. It made more sense to me than the human world. I understood my little dog better that the complexities of my parents."

Among his early literary influences were Benjamin Radier, creator of "La Vache Qui Rit" ("The Laughing Cow"), who specialized in smiling animals. "He did marvelous comic strips with lots of humor, laughing hares, and

smiling geese. Also, of course, Babar—those books were first published around the time I was born." Annaud also recalls seeing enchanting lithographs by the nineteenth-century artist Jean Ignace Isidore Gerard Grandville, who drew fanciful genre scenes of animals in human garb and situations, "a sort of pre-Darwinian approach.

"From those early days I retained great sympathy and, I believe, understanding for four-legged beings," Annaud says. "It's a world in which I feel very comfortable." The director's second home is an old mill in Brittany where he and his wife, continuity supervisor Laurence Duval-Annaud, live with dogs, geese, donkeys, and rabbits. "It is where I 'grew' this movie. I need this kind of environment. Especially after *Enemy at the Gates*, which was about war and fire and blood, I felt the need to go back to the tropical forest and the innocence of animals. I never want to start a movie without knowing where my soul is, where my feelings are. I feel strongly that my life is informed by the movies I make, therefore the choices I make are in direct connection with my needs. Making films is a search to enter another kind of consciousness, and if one is oriented toward animals and nature, that is a direction you want to explore."

Hand-colored wood engraving by Grandville, "Ses manieres étaient celles d'un Chat" ("His manners were those of a cat"), 1842. From the series: Scenes from the Private and Public Lives of Animals. Davidson Galleries.

A career, in short, that never strayed far from Annaud's childhood passions and preoccupations, and whose extraordinary achievements were fueled by that core philosophy: "Everything is possible." A career leading, finally, to a film that blended these passions as none had before: *Two Brothers*, an enthralling tale of tigers, men, and temples; of discovery, survival, and wonder, set in the jungles of colonial Indochina, circa early 1900s.

"I wanted the story to be reminiscent of the fables I loved so much as a child," explains Annaud. "It is constructed upon the wondrous imaginative references of children—the jungle, the mysterious ruins, the golden palace, the world of animals, the circus. The characters have one foot in the real world and one foot in fairy tales: the rich child, the hunter, the beautiful native girl, the prince and his fiancée, the dignitary and his ambitious wife, the animal tamer.

"This movie combines three of my greatest passions: the animal world; a love of monasteries and temples, and my fascination with the European colonial period," Annaud concludes.

"To this day, that first visit to Cambodia remains the artistic shock of my life. I just could not believe the combination of religious devotion and sheer artistic beauty. The romanticism of it all was fascinating. The forest's revenge on man. The trees strangling the stones."

—JEAN-JACQUES ANNAUD

"View of the great road which leads to Ponteoy Pracan," engraving by Louis Delaporte from Voyage d'Exploration en Indochine, *by Francis Garnier, 1873.*

Filmmaking and the Path of Desire

The path that brought Annaud to *Two Brothers* is clear enough in hindsight, though he often felt as if he was finding his way through a tangled jungle. After film school and a brief detour into the military (which he spent in French colonial West Africa), Annaud plunged into the world of advertising, making more than 500 commercials and winning many industry awards thanks to his witty, visually iconoclastic style. Eight years down this glittering road, at the top of his field, he crashed in a severe depression—from which he emerged in dawning realization that he didn't care about what he was doing; that he was skating on the surface of his talent; that what he really wanted more than anything was to direct a feature film.

He didn't need to look far for his story: *Black and White in Color* grew out of his own experience in West Africa and—typical of all Annaud projects since—his extensive reading about the place and period. It's the story of a handful of French colonials in Cameroon in 1915, who enjoy congenial relations with Germans in a nearby military outpost until they discover their homelands are at war. Released in 1976, it comments with a light touch on war, racism, and ruling-class hubris. The fate of *Black and White in Color* took a strange turn when it was submitted for Academy Award consideration not by France, but by the Ivory Coast. It went on to win the Oscar for Best Foreign Language Film in 1977, exposing Annaud to his first white-hot flash of fame.

Annaud sees clear links between his earliest and latest films: "I discovered the world of the colonials in Africa and learned more about it from researching *Black and White in Color*. They lose contact with their own world and create another world. They have power but are extremely isolated. They live in a sort of luxury but usually in countries where it's very warm—where there's nothing to do, nowhere to go, and no roads to get there. And they cannot avoid experiencing the power of nature. I find this whole situation fascinating."

ABOVE: Guy Pearce, Freddie Highmore, Philippine Leroy-Beaulieu, and Jean-Claude Dreyfus portray the colonials in Two Brothers. *OPPOSITE: Guy Pearce.*

Beyond Words

"Movies are made to be seen, not to be heard." This could serve as a manifesto for Jean-Jacques Annaud's approach to filmmaking. "Our job as filmmakers is to show the drama, to make you understand it visually. Of course we can put in the sound. But first we are visual people. Dialogue is the sound of man, but sometimes it's less important than music or the storm in the background or the birds in the forest."

Having made one movie with only four or five lines of dialogue (*The Bear*) and another in which the characters speak an invented language when they speak at all (*Quest for Fire*), Annaud has practiced what he preaches. "Compared to some of my other movies, *Two Brothers* has a lot of scenes with dialogue. But very often scripts are overwritten. Too many words to explain too many things. If you have to explain what the film is about, what's the point of making the movie?

"I love making images that convey the characters' feelings. Shooting with actors who can act instead of say. And dealing with situations that can be understood without too many subtitles. When I'm writing a screenplay, I describe what I see. This is probably why I like working with animals so much. If I write: 'The tiger is roaming in the forest, hears a noise, climbs on a rock, sees in the distance creatures he's never seen,' do I need words? Does the tiger need to say, 'Oh, dear, this is a strange noise that I'm hearing. What are those creatures?' No; I just need a little zoom on the eyes and the two ears twitching. And you get it."

Annaud uses his computer to "season" his printed screenplays with found illustrations as visual aids to his crew and actors. They may provide inspiration for sets, costumes, or situations, and he used the device in *Two Brothers* to compensate for the lack of dialogue. "So much of the story is visual, especially what is told through the tigers' behavior. Since they don't speak, I had to indicate somehow that their faces and bodies can express whatever is going on. People using the script learn that you can identify with the animals and know what they think just by looking at their eyes."

The "less is more" approach works with human actors, too, Annaud feels. He was happy to discover that Guy Pearce, his human lead in *Two Brothers*, prefers working this way. "He knows that the less he says and the more he plays, the more intriguing it is. The joy of working with an actor like him is that he loves to have less dialogue and play what is not written."

"In *Two Brothers*, the French governor Normandin and his family are very typical of displaced colonial people. I see this film as the offspring of both *Black and White in Color*, in that it is set in the colonial world, and *The Bear*, in telling the story from the animals' point of view."

Annaud's second effort was *Coup de Tête (Hothead)*, which centers on a failing soccer player who becomes an unlikely hero by scoring the decisive goal in a big match for his team and town. This small film did respectably, but it was Annaud's next project that firmly established him in the ranks of international directors to watch.

Quest for Fire was conceived with screenwriter Gérard Brach, who shared Annaud's fascination with prehistoric humans. Finding funding for this unique, risky production proved just the first of many massive challenges that only Annaud's stubborn confidence and improvisational skills carried him past. Audiences around the world responded to his imaginative re-creation of the world of our distant ancestors, with its only "dialogue" a language invented for the film by novelist Anthony Burgess (*A Clockwork Orange*). Released in 1981, *Quest for Fire* displays many Annaud trademarks: his fearlessness at tackling big themes, his use of spectacular natural backdrops, and above all his reliance on visual storytelling rather than dialogue.

It was Gérard Brach who brought Annaud the book that would become their next project, and the direct precursor to *Two Brothers*. When Annaud read *The Grizzly King*, a nearly-forgotten novel by Michigan writer James Oliver Curwood (and a childhood favorite of Brach), his own early love for animal tales burst into

"Throughout my career I have had the privilege to do all the movies I wanted to make, and only the movies I wanted to make. What is it I would change?"

—*JEAN-JACQUES ANNAUD*

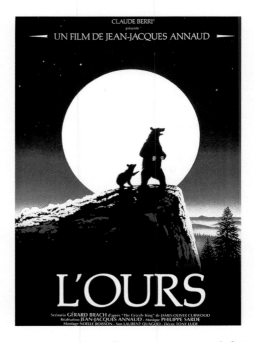

flame. What most appealed to him and challenged him about the story was that the animals were the protagonists; the story was told almost entirely from the point of view of two grizzlies: a powerful old male and the orphaned cub he reluctantly adopts.

The Bear was not a nature documentary but rather a three-act work of dramatic fiction—scripted, rehearsed, and acted by a cast in which the principals were willful, nonverbal, and dangerous carnivores. Eschewing conventional voiceover narration, Annaud cinematically transported moviegoers into the raw essence of the wild, presenting the animals' day-to-day lives from their perspective. He even dared to visually imagine what these animals might dream about.

Everywhere *The Bear* opened, starting with its October 1988 debut in France, it was embraced by audiences and critics. *Newsweek* reviewer David Ansen called the film "audacious . . . unique and enchanting" and commented, "No small part of the film's fascination is wondering how on earth the filmmakers achieved these results." *Time* magazine's Richard Schickel observed, "*The Bear* is to other films about nature what *Star Wars* was to science-fiction movies: a redefinition of the state of the art."

Making *The Bear* turned out to be a seven-year odyssey and posed production problems that no previous filmmaker ever had to solve. Locations had to be identified that closely resembled the bears' native habitat of British Columbia and satisfied Annaud's vision of the story's landscape, yet were affordable and logistically accessible. Solutions had to be found in scripting and storyboarding to making the action clear without help from words. Real grizzly actors had to be cast as the two lead bears (including the cub at various ages), as well as two female "supporting actors"; then they and their trainers had to be safely transported, housed, and cared

for during the shoot. Since there were limits to what real animals could be asked to do, the filmmakers had to research and devise ways to use human mimes and mechanical ("animatronic" bears) in some scenes.

Above all, the director and trainers had to find ways to elicit behavior and emotional responses from their animals that would form the core of their performance. This was the film's key accomplishment, what set it apart from any other movie about animals to date. These same challenges came up for Annaud again in *Two Brothers*, and despite recent technological advances that enabled him to solve some problems in

ABOVE: *Movie poster for the original French release of* The Bear (L'Ours). RIGHT: *Still photo from* Quest for Fire.

Tiger Eyes

"When I was researching *The Bear*, I actually was not sure at first what animal I would be dealing with," says Annaud. "I went to the zoo many times to figure out which animal the audience could best identify with.

"I was instinctively attracted to tigers and especially fascinated with their eyes, but I was afraid they were too different from humans. Because bears were vertical beings very often, like humans, I thought they would be easiest for people to identify with. After the movie was released, I realized that didn't have anything to do with it—it was simply much easier than I had imagined for an audience to relate to nonhuman creatures. At that point, my main regret was passing up an animal with wonderful eyes. A bear's nose is quite expressive, always moving, because they rely on scent. But they don't have good eyes or good eyesight.

"Tigers have the most amazing eyes because they are predators who relate to the world primarily through sight. This is why they have so much expression and why you can so easily read in their eyes what they see, what they feel, what they want. This became central to the film.

"After three weeks of shooting I was panicking because I realized that I could not use just any closeup of a tiger looking in a certain direction—even if it was the right direction. It also had to have the right expression for the scene. Unlike bears, tigers always have an expression of some kind, depending on what their eyes, mouth, and ears are doing. Much like a human actor, you cannot just use any shot of him looking right or left. There must be the appropriate expression on his face."

new ways, his basic approach remained the same: to build character portrayals around the animal's natural emotions and behaviors, with which we humans can closely identify.

"It was actually during my research for *Quest For Fire* that I discovered how much we share with animals: body language, behavior," says Annaud. "That's why we understand when an animal is angry or pleased or sad."

One reason *The Bear*'s journey to the screen took so long was that simultaneously Annaud was developing a script for *The Name of the Rose*, with the help of Gérard Brach and co-writer Alain Godard. In fact, *The Name of the Rose* was shot and released first—Annaud wanted to show the public a different side of his talent after *Quest for Fire*; to work with humans actors and dialogue in a "civilized" setting.

Throughout the next decade, Annaud's projects continued to stretch his filmmaking muscles while staying faithful to his passions: from his evocative adaptation of Marguerite Duras's prize-winning novel *The Lover*, in which the illicit lovers communicate far more with looks and action than with words; to the groundbreaking IMAX spectacle *Wings of Courage*, based on a story by Annaud's compatriot Antoine de Saint-Exupéry, with its spectacular Andean mountain scenery. *Seven Years in Tibet*, starring Brad Pitt, gave Annaud the chance to explore another ancient monastic world, Lhasa circa 1900. And the World War II drama *Enemy at the Gates* showed that he could hold his own with any director at staging battle scenes on a vast scale, while focusing his story on the tense, strangely intimate relationship between two snipers on opposing sides in the siege of Stalingrad.

The Genesis of *Two Brothers*

With *Two Brothers*, Annaud revisits the animal kingdom for the first time since *The Bear*. Imprinted with animal stories as a child, he finds endless fascination in exploring the lives and emotional worlds of complex, intelligent creatures. Learning as an adult about the real biological and psychic connections between humans and animals only intensified his interest. "I must have read about three hundred books on animal behavior, and they are absolutely fascinating—particularly those about animal perception, sexual behavior, communication, and even dreaming."

In exploring story ideas, the filmmaker was particularly intrigued by the notion of long-term memory in these animals. "I am surprised that most humans feel so superior that they rule out any intelligence, memory and emotions in other species. People who live closely with dogs or cats cannot fail to acknowledge these abilities. I don't believe that it is being anthropomorphic but, in fact, having a greater understanding of the depths of animal intelligence."

Recent experiments have led scientists—who have long maintained the absence in animals of so-called episodic memory, the kind that allows humans to recall past events—to rethink the nature of memory in animals.

ABOVE: Poster designed for set decoration of Two Brothers.

A 2003 story in *National Geographic Today* cites several experts on animal behavior who are challenging old-fashioned notions regarding animal memory. Says one of them, psychologist John Pearce, "We have traditionally regarded animals like machines, or automata, believing that they just have reflexes and habits. [This new] work is revolutionary because it . . . suggests that animals have richer memories than previously thought."

Annaud admits to feeling a special affinity for tigers, "Even before I made *The Bear*," he says, "I had trouble deciding whether to make a film featuring bears or tigers. Although the bears were wonderful, I always regretted that I didn't use the splendid majesty of the tigers. So I was thrilled to finally have the opportunity."

He came up with the basic framework of the story, he says, to amuse himself and his family during a vacation in remote southern Yemen. "We would all go to bed inside the tent, and I said to myself, why don't I just write a little story? I came up with this one."

Many details of the story remained to be filled in, but Annaud always knew that his setting would be Southeast Asia. A side trip to Cambodia during his promotion work for *The Lover* (set in Vietnam) gave Annaud his first direct experience of the magical Angkor Temples.

"My wife and I first visited Cambodia in 1989," says Annaud. "The temples were full of land mines so we had to get special permission to go there. To this day, that visit remains the artistic shock of my life."

In characterizing *Two Brothers*, Annaud comes back again and again to terms like "fable" and "fairy tale." As in most fairy tales, the exact time is left unspecified, although for Annaud the romance and mystery of the Indochinese temples are associated with the period when they were first discovered by Europeans: the late 19th and early 20th centuries. This time frame also offered the opportunity to explore the colonial milieu he knows so well.

"When an opportunity to do a film comes, I always have to ask myself: am I passionate enough about this project to live with it for three years? Will I fight for it? And if I can't answer yes, I can't do the film."

—*JEAN-JACQUES ANNAUD*

Beyond the where and when, we move into the territory of children's tales. In the movie's story of sibling tiger cubs who lose their parents, become separated, grow into different fates, and finally reunite, the elements are classic. How many tales feature a young hero who is orphaned or abducted into a strange, cruel environment? How many stories tell of brothers and sisters, or twins, who are very different in their character and destinies? Annaud and Godard are working in this genre, and the director also notes recent research about the roles of "nature versus nurture" in talking about the divergent paths of Kumal and Sangha:

"I've always been fascinated by twins, especially by twins that are separated. What is it in each of us that comes from our nature, from our genetic heritage, and what comes from education and knowledge? There are so many accounts of twins whose lives seem fated to follow the same path, even if they are separated. The story here is of two twins, or at least siblings, that are separated soon after birth, and reunited in a very dramatic moment, a combat for life."

Each pair of tiger cubs that portrayed Kumal and Sangha in *Two Brothers* came from the same litter but showed distinct personality differences. "We see their different personalities very early in the film, while they are still together: Kumal is bolder, the dominant one; Sangha more timid. But then we see how those basic traits are affected by what happens to them in captivity. The dominant cub becomes a circus animal, but because it is always bored, it loses its personality and energy, while the more fearful and shy one becomes very ferocious in captivity. This is usually the case: trainers observe that the most ferocious tigers are the ones who are frightened of everything, which makes them more aggressive. Still, when our tigers finally meet again, they recognize each other."

It was important that the movie contain a child's perspective, so the character of young Raoul, the son of the governor Normandin, is pivotal. Through Raoul we experience the excitement of living in a strange land where tigers, elephants, monkeys, and bejeweled royalty are facts of life. Through his love for Sangha, we share a no-holds-barred expression of the enormous attraction people feel for baby animals, and the heartbreak of learning that some creatures cannot be part of the human world. In his hero-worship of the great hunter, McRory, we're reminded of the storybook heroes of our youth.

"As in every fable," Annaud comments, "there is a moral to the story: what happens when we take these animals out of the wild and keep them in captivity?" He explains, "There are many people who keep tigers in their back yards. If you found an abandoned tiger cub, you too would be enamored with it and would want to keep it. You would want to take it home. However, what do you do when it becomes full grown? The tiger is a predator. No matter how much you love the animal, it is very dangerous. That's its nature."

Two Writers, One Mind

Like most innovative directors, Jean-Jacques Annaud is closely involved with writing his film stories, thriving on the collaboration with gifted screenwriters. Before bringing in Alain Godard to work on *Two Brothers*, though, he needed to lay the groundwork. Annaud himself produced a 25-page sketch, then a 100-page rough screenplay, just to see where the story might go. "I gave him just the 25 pages and kept the longer version as a guide for our conversation. The final script, after six drafts, was very different.

"Most of the time when I get a script, I don't understand it," he says in explaining his approach. "I often see fabulous scripts that end up on the screen as wonderful movies, but I have no regrets—I could not do what those directors have done because I did not understand the characters or the story. I have always been involved in the writing."

Whenever possible, Annaud and Godard work together in person, in the same room, trading plot ideas and lines, revising and polishing, until they are content with the result.

"It works very well," says Annaud happily. "I type, he sits in an armchair, and we just describe the scene between the two of us. One will say a line, the other adds an adjective, then the first comes up with a line of dialogue. At the end of the day, we don't remember whose idea was whose. We have very long days, starting at nine in the morning, ending at nine in the evening; we take a one-hour break for lunch at a little restaurant near my house.

"On this movie we wrote almost everything together, then I moved to Cambodia and we communicated on later revisions by email and phone."

Each collaborator brings different strengths to the task, says Annaud. "Alain has a wonderful sense of humor and a great ease with language. He is also a great self-critic and is never tired of doing it again. For him, as for me, it's never finished, never good enough. For this movie, we consciously worked to create contrast between the serious and the ridiculous— the fate of the tigers set against the comedy of the human colonialists."

Godard recalls working on the scene in *Two Brothers* where the mother tiger chases a truck carrying one of her cubs down the road, leaping on the back to try to free him. "I was quite relieved that I didn't have to direct it myself!" But this was totally in character for Annaud, he says. "It might happen that Jean-Jacques would refuse a script idea because he finds it too flashy, or too fake—but *never* because it is impossible."

Jean-Jacques Annaud goes over a script revision while on location in Cambodia.

The Production Family

After dashing off the germ of the *Two Brothers* story on holiday, Annaud let the idea lie fallow for several years while engaged with other projects. When he felt ready to move forward, he first took as much time as he needed to assure himself that the film he dreamed of could be made: "I met with tiger experts, went to see trainer Thierry Le Portier and saw his tigers, did all my reading."

Next, he gathered the core team of collaborators who would help him make it, beginning with screenwriter Alain Godard. One of the director's oldest friends—both began their careers in advertising—Godard had earlier collaborated on the screenplays for *Quest for Fire, The Name of the Rose, Wings of Courage,* and *Enemy at the Gates.* Godard's other writing credits include *La Femme du Cosmonaute, Palace, Signes Extérieurs de Richesse,* and *It's Not Me, It's Him.* Annaud and Godard began writing the screenplay for *Two Brothers* in 1999.

Another of the first people Annaud contacted about *Two Brothers* was producer Jake Eberts, one of the most active independent film producers in the industry. The two first worked together in 1985 when Eberts co-financed and executive-produced *The Name of the Rose.* Other notable films with which Eberts has been associated as producer or executive producer include *Watership Down, The Howling, Chariots of Fire, Local Hero, Gandhi, The Killing Fields, The Dresser, Hope and Glory, Driving Miss Daisy, Dances with Wolves, A River Runs Through It,* and *Open Range.* Eberts also serves on the board of the Sundance Institute.

"It was the beginning of a great friendship," says Eberts of his first collaboration with Annaud. "We stayed in touch over the years, and in 1998 Jean-Jacques outlined his idea to make a film about tigers set in the temples of Southeast Asia. I loved everything about it. It is exactly my kind of movie. It has

Jean-Jacques Annaud and Jake Eberts (right) confer on the set.

"When Jean-Jacques outlined his idea to make a film about tigers set in the temples of Southeast Asia, I loved everything about it. It is exactly my kind of movie. It has history, animal conservation, preservation of culture and the environment, and on top of that, a great story. I was hooked from the beginning."

—*PRODUCER JAKE EBERTS*

history, animal conservation, preservation of culture and the environment, and on top of that, a great story. I was hooked from the beginning. From there it snowballed into one of the most challenging projects I have ever worked on."

Two Brothers also reunited Annaud with several longtime members of his creative family, including line producer Xavier Castano, whom the director credits for keeping things running smoothly on the film's remote, difficult locations; editor Noelle Boisson, who has collaborated with Annaud on three previous pictures; animal trainer Thierry Le Portier, who worked with him on *The Bear*; and production designer Pierre Queffelean, who was his art director on *Seven Years in Tibet* and made the leap to head of production design with this film.

Annaud, with his unique background and a veteran team to support him in every detail, was in an ideal position to live out this filmmaking adventure. As always, before beginning production he immersed himself in his topic—in this case the natural history and lore of tigers, and their perilous place in today's world. "It takes me a year to write any film because I need at least six months of research, then at least six months of writing, and then of course pre-production—scouting for locations and casting and all. But I enjoy that process."

All this homework, Annaud believed, would help him tell a story that was rooted not just in his imagination but in the tiger's own world.

"I love to identify with animals. I love thinking that I could be a bird or a fish. So with tigers, I wanted to try to enter their experience as much as possible," he says. "I regret that not many movies or books tell stories from the point of view of an animal in a serious and entertaining way. In a documentary you learn facts, but you may not really understand why an animal acts as it does. I am trying to give the audience a new way of looking at animals. And to make people dream.

"All the different elements in my life led me to this story."

BELOW: *Filmmaking, animals, and ancient temples come together in the making of* Two Brothers.

"Jean-Jacques might refuse a script idea because he finds it too flashy, or too fake—but *never* because it is impossible."

—SCREENWRITER ALAIN GODARD

The Way of the Tiger

What is it about tigers that impelled Jean-Jacques Annaud to create a film story around them? Begin with his childhood love for animals of all kinds; his ability—like that of many only children who grow up with few same-age playmates—to make a direct emotional connection with a pet dog. Add the magic of childhood tales featuring marvelous animals and the impact of seeing exotic creatures face to face at the zoo—creatures that had existed only in his imagination or in illustrated books and comics. Combine these early influences with a filmmaker's drive to conjure new worlds on the screen, and making films about animals isn't so surprising.

"The attraction we feel to animals, the need we feel to have a dog, a cat—why is that?" Annaud wonders. "Because part of the brain feels comfortable with other creatures that are very much like us, but because they don't speak, are both a mystery and a relief."

And tigers are among a handful of animals that set the human imagination on fire, creatures extraordinary enough to compete with the imagined beasts of fiction and fantasy. They are among what naturalist writer David Quammen calls "monsters of God" or "alpha predators"—the top carnivores of every continent on Earth, beasts powerful and bold enough to kill human beings. Animals that make us aware we are not alone at the top of the food chain, that indeed, we may from time to time be relegated to prey. Animals whose very presence, even if unseen, keeps jungles and forests as wild, dark, and scary as they are painted in fairytales.

In modern times we have tried hard to tame the tiger and turn it for our uses: Esso gasoline for years was sold by the slogan "Put a tiger in your tank!" and the cartoon Tony the Tiger is still selling breakfast cereal. But the real tiger always evades such control sooner or later. A. A. Milne delighted children with

> **F**or the people who lived under the umbrella of the forest, the tiger was the most important, most powerful representation of nature that walked the earth. Nature was the giver of life, and the tiger seemed to symbolize the force that could provide life, defeat evil, and act as an "elder brother" to man, defending crops and driving out unhealthy spirits. It was the protector, the guardian, the intermediary between heaven and earth....
>
> All this is irrespective of the fact that tigers sometimes killed people, long before the arrival of the professional hunter. Forest communities accepted the tiger's right to intervene in their lives—that which gave life also had the right to take it away.
>
> —VALMIK THAPAR, THE TIGER'S DESTINY

OPPOSITE: Maharaja Umed Singh of Kotah shooting a tiger. *Kotah school, c. 1790. Victoria & Albert Museum, London.*

the engaging Tigger in his Pooh stories, but the unpredictable striped beast always made his fellow characters a little edgy. And the compelling image from a famous children's tale is of the brave boy Sambo taking refuge in a tree while tigers relentlessly circle below.

Wherever in the world tigers have lived—and their range once extended from Mesopotamia to the Arctic, from Java to the Black Sea—people have recognized in them a powerful life force, a creature that dominates its world as humans in the past could only wish to. Among certain tribes of Siberia, the tiger was revered as the guardian of the forest;

in northeastern India, a legend relates that the first tiger and the first man on earth were brothers, born of the same spirit. The name of the Tigris River comes from the old tale of a tiger who appeared at a crucial moments and bore a princess across the raging river on his back. Parts of the tiger's body were thought to carry magic: its whiskers gave power over women; its penis made the best aphrodisiac; tiger fat relieved aches and pains; its teeth and claws conferred power and turned back evil. (Unfortunately, such beliefs persist, and tigers are still dying for them.)

In past millennia, tigers were just as dangerous to

man as they are today, yet people of the forest accepted this relationship with a powerful equal, and made magic from it. Even today this impulse survives here and there. In the mountains of Sumatra, the Kerinci people hold a dualistic view: they fear the physical tiger, which they call *harimau biasa*; but they also believe in a spirit tiger, called *harimau roh*, who is seen as an ancestral guardian and whose energy they try to invoke when threatened.

THIS PAGE: Annaud's location scouting photos show the tiger's influence in Southeast Asia. OPPOSITE: Nai-Rea (Mai Anh Le) and her brother, who lost a leg to a tiger, in a still from the film.

But though there are far fewer tigers and far more people today, that old bond is broken. The people who must live close to tigers today, in the rural villages of South Asia, are mostly agriculturists, not hunters. To them the tiger is not a respected coequal in the pursuit of food on the hoof. Nor can they admire the tiger's beauty and power from afar, like we in developed nations who support preserving such endangered creatures. To these people, tigers are deadly shadows that lurk on the dark edges of their cleared fields, now and then carrying off precious livestock and maiming or killing a villager. Little wonder that they fear and hate tigers.

"I do hope there will still be some space for animals in the wild, and I believe in working for that," says Annaud. "But it is easy for me, living in an apartment in Paris, to say to people in Cambodia: You should have wild tigers in your back yard. But people in the villages where we shot the film hate tigers, because the tigers go into their village, get their pigs, get their buffaloes, even get their kids sometimes.

"In this part of the world tigers are perceived to be as bad as wolves were in the middle ages in Europe. There is an interspecies conflict here. In the film, the character of Nai-Rea, the young woman who translates for McRory, expresses how her people feel about tigers.

"Still," the director concludes, "I believe that it's good for the human species to share this planet with plants, birds, fish, mammals, tigers, bears, rabbits, butterflies. We come from the animal world, and if we are the only creature alive in a few decades, it's a very sad world."

"If we address him as 'Tiger,' he will eat us; if we address him as 'Mr. Tiger,' he will eat us."

— *HINDU PROVERB*

Tigers in the Wild

What is the reality of this splendid creature that has occupied so much space in our imagination? How do tigers live in nature, and how do they respond to captivity? These were questions Annaud had to explore; fairytale or no, it was important to him that the film be truthful in how it depicts the tiger's nature. Moreover, he was working with real tigers, which behave according to their nature even when raised in captivity—so the images on screen reflect how tigers actually perceive and react. If the story ran contrary to what audiences saw, there would be a serious disconnect. Audiences would not engage emotionally with the characters.

"At it's heart, it's the story of twins that get separated. When we meet them, they're just cubs living happily in the jungle, in the ruins of temples that have been left to decay in the middle of the forest. This is inspired by reality—tigers love to den inside rocky caves and can be found in ruins. In India, for instance, there's a remarkable wildlife park where you can see wild tigers around an ancient fort." (See sidebar, "The Tigers of Ranthambhore," about the Indian reserve where tigers casually incorporate the ruins of human civilization into their habitat.)

Before humans ever enter the frame in *Two Brothers*, we are introduced to a family of tigers living very much as wild tiger families live anywhere—except that their jungle home includes the fabulous temples of Angkor. The family unit consists of a mother and two cubs: a typical number, though three is also common. The mother may carry and bear more young, but most do not survive the first few days of life. Gestation takes just over three months, and a tigress does not show her pregnancy until very late.

LEFT: One of the film's tigers prowls amid the ruins of Preah Khan temple. OPPOSITE: A wild tiger at Ranthambore Fort in India's Ranthambhore National Park. Photo by Valmik Thapar/Peter Arnold.

The Tigers of Ranthambhore

A highlight of Annaud's research for *Two Brothers* was a visit to India's Ranthambhore National Park and Tiger Reserve, in eastern Rajasthan. Perhaps no other place on earth is so closely associated with tigers and tiger conservation. One of the original nine reserves established in 1972 by Project Tiger—a collaborative effort by the Indian government, the World Wildlife Fund, and the World Conservation Union—Ranthambhore has been the site of groundbreaking field research into the tiger's lifeways, as well as experiments such as relocating local people outside the reserve boundaries to reduce conflict with tigers. Project Tiger has had a rocky history and faces grave problems in maintaining stable tiger populations—but there's little doubt it was responsible for bringing the Bengal tiger subspecies back from the brink of extinction to its current number of between 4,000 and 5,000 animals.

The man mostly closely linked with tigers at Ranthambhore is the dedicated researcher, author, and documentary filmmaker Valmik Thapar, author of the classic *Tiger: Portrait of a Predator* and other books. As the first stop on his research trail, Annaud spent two weeks in the reserve with Thapar, soaking up his deep knowledge of all things tiger. "Valmik is a great friend who helped me to understand tiger behavior through our long conversations and his wonderful books," says Annaud.

Ranthambhore's natural beauty and diversity are impressive enough, but it also contains the ruin of 1,000-year-old Ranthambhore Fort, atop a high hill at the heart of the park. Crumbling stone cenotaphs, tombs, stepped wells, summer palaces—all have merged harmoniously into the sprawling forest. To the Ranthambhore tigers, the structures are just part of their habitat: good perches for observing what lies below, or just for an afternoon snooze—they have often been photographed sprawled across the stones.

To Annaud, this discovery came with a startling sense of déjà vu, as he had already imagined the tiger characters in his screenplay living among such ruins in Indochina. Seeing it in the flesh confirmed that his story line was not just feasible but quite natural for any tigers whose territory happened to include such long-abandoned structures. "I may have seen pictures of Ranthambhore long ago and forgotten about them," he speculates. "But in any case it was good confirmation of what I had already written."

Tiger, tiger, burning bright
In the forests of the night;
What immortal hand or eye
Could frame thy fearful symmetry?

—WILLIAM BLAKE

Tigers are solitary except during mating or when raising cubs. (In most cases, the female is the assertive partner; mating takes place at her choice.) A tigress in heat vocalizes insistently until a male responds, and male and female spend several days together during mating—usually the only time in an adult tiger's life when it enjoys such companionship. When they mate, the forest resounds with their roars, aggression alternating with tenderness as the partners nuzzle and cuddle each other, or lash out periodically. The pair may mate many times in just an hour or so—up to eight times has been observed.

When the time comes, cubs are born in dense forest, concealing grass, or some other secure den. Like the young of other cats, they are blind and helpless at birth; the first few weeks are critical, and

Tigers live an intense social life, but at one remove, like hermits who spend all their lives on the telephone. They know all about their neighbors and what they are up to. They know who they are, their age and their sex and, if with active cubs, how many. They know where their neighbors have been. Tigers will know as individuals all the tigers whose territories abut their own. The complex territorial patterns of males and females are all conveyed through smell. Information is constantly exchanged through the jungle by the silent gossip of scent. Tigers are everlastingly curious about each other, yet they seldom meet."

— SIMON BARNES, TIGER!

the mother will move the cubs if she senses any disturbance. Carrying them across open ground is a risky maneuver, as the film depicts. As the cubs grow, the devoted mother spends as much time with them as possible, frequently licking and cleaning them, leaving the den only to hunt. Cubs live on mother's milk for their first three months, then begin to chew on bits of meat she brings back.

Observers are unfailingly touched by the obvious closeness and affection in tiger families. As fellow mammals who nurse and carefully tend our young, we recognize this bond instantly. And nature has endowed baby tigers with can't-miss appeal, whether to their own mothers or to humans who encounter them. The film's plot turns on this appeal, and it was a constant feature of life on the set, where everyone wanted to feed and play with the cubs. Actor Guy Pearce, whose role called for him to handle the cubs a lot, fell under their spell completely. "It was an astounding experience every day. I couldn't put them down. We'd finish a take and the trainer would come running over to say 'I'll relieve you of the tiger,' and I'm saying, no, no, it's okay."

This family unit endures for about two years, for it takes young tigers at least this long to learn to fend for themselves. As solitary hunters, each must be able to stalk, kill, and defend prey—enough of it to sustain a full-grown tiger weighing hundreds of pounds. Acquiring these skills takes a long time and much careful tutelage on the mother's part.

When cubs are a few months old, their mother takes them out exploring, an important first step in learning the language of their environment. At first she keep in close physical touch with them, as they are vulnerable to many perils, including other predators. She exerts firm discipline; their survival depends on learning caution and patience. The film shows the early adventures of Kumal and Sangha in charming sequences. "Basically they are tigers in the wild, they play all the time," notes Annaud. "We see them with their mother, playing with her tail, with coconut shells and small animals, swimming, climbing trees ..."

Quite early, tiger siblings begin to show differences in personality. One will tend to dominate and take the lead in investigating new experiences. In the film, this is clearly Kumal, who

OPPOSITE: Indra, a trained tigress used in the film, was very tolerant of cubs that were not hers. BELOW: The cub portraying Sangha in a stand-off with a civet cat.

"Some form of sibling bond seems to last into adulthood. I think the tigers of Ranthambhore . . . sustain kin links."

—VALMIK THAPAR,
THE TIGER'S DESTINY

stands his ground in a confrontation with an angry civet cat after Sangha has backed down. "When we did the scene with the civet, we just played it according to how the cubs behaved," says Annaud. "The dominant sibling of this pair of cubs was not frightened, while the other was frightened and ran away. Faced with that very aggressive little animal, the two of them had entirely different reactions—as if they had read the script!"

The film faithfully depicts tiger family life, with one unusual twist: the male tiger who sired Kumal and Sangha is shown joining the family for a siesta and play session by the river where they all cool off. This is not the norm for tigers—males of this species, like other wild felines, often kill their offspring to preclude competition for territory, or simply ignore them. But peaceful interaction is not unknown. During his visit to Ranthambhore, Annaud did encounter lasting family groups. "The males visit the females," he relates "hunt with them, play with the young, share their prey, or protect the family from possible dangers." This little-known aspect of tiger social life inspired several scenes in *Two Brothers*.

> A stalking tiger uses every available piece of cover. It approaches cautiously, carefully, placing each foot on the ground. It crouches behind small bushes or rocks, or hugs the edge of a riverbank, all the while remaining focused on the prey. With its striped coat effectively breaking up its outline, the tiger moves slowly forward, patiently closing the distance or waiting for the prey to move closer. Having got to within 10 to 20 meters or less of the prey, the tiger gathers itself up and suddenly rushes its victim, covering the final distance in a few bounds."
>
> —MEL SUNQUIST AND FIONA C. SUNQUIST, *GREAT CATS*

As the cubs get bigger, their mother must hunt more intensively to feed them. They begin to travel more widely with her, and to stalk and hunt small prey. Near-constant play develops the cubs' strength, agility, and hunting reflexes, and confirms dominance patterns. Later they start trying to help the tigress hunt, though not very usefully. The mother-cub relationship changes over time, the tigress showing increasingly less patience with the cubs.

Older cubs eventually begin to range out on their own or in pairs, even while still dependent on mom. At this point, the tigress spends more and more time away from them, and finally they venture forth to stake out their own territories. As the young tiger starts to hunt larger prey, it will fail most of the time but gradually hones its skills to become a fully competent predator. And there is no more powerful or skillful hunter on the planet then a mature tiger, who can bring down a water buffalo twice its own weight. Success usually depends on a stealthy

RIGHT: *The tiger family together during filming by the Kbal Spean River.*

Another disruptive factor [in Siberian tiger populations in Soviet Russia] was the live capture of cubs and juveniles for sale to the world's zoos, among whom the very rarity of P. t. altaica made it a desirable acquisition. The live capture trade was brisk in several villages along the Bolshaya Ussurka River. . . . Within those villages, expert tiger trappers emerged from certain families of hunters. . . . They used dogs to track a tiger cub and corner it, forked poles to pin it down, and tough fabric to shackle its paws, and by one account they managed a good record of not breaking cubs' teeth. But kidnapping young tigers was a frenetic process, whatever the technique, and sometimes it entailed killing a protective mother. . . . Extracting cub from the wild could scarcely be done without serious harm to the adult population.

— DAVID QUAMMEN, MONSTERS OF GOD

stalk followed by a powerful leap, as tigers are too heavy for long chases.

In the case of Kumal and Sangha in *Two Brothers*, this peaceful progression toward adulthood is tragically interrupted when they are quite small. "One day men come to their unknown paradise," Annaud relates. "This is when the tragedy happens, when they are captured and separated. In our story, the male tiger gets killed while defending his territory. The mother escapes with one baby and leaves the other for a few seconds—but in those few seconds he is captured by a hunter and later sold to a circus.

"The other cub is captured later on, while the mother is hunted. This is very often what happened in reality; even today you find cubs on the market in some places of Asia, because the mother has been killed." Later in the film, the young tigers meet again, and though they are intended to fight, they instead make peace. There is no direct source for such a scenario in the life of wild tigers, but researchers have been surprised to see grown tigers interact peacefully and theorize that it is because they recognize each other as kin.

One inescapable reality is that wild tigers need a lot of space. A single tiger's home range can vary from 50 to 1,000 square kilometers for the Bengal subspecies and 500 to 4,000 square kilometers for the Siberian subspecies, where prey tends to be more spread out. A male's range may overlap with that of several females, but considerable numbers of each gender are needed to maintain a healthy gene pool. These facts of tiger life bring it into direct conflict with the vectors of human history: our relentlessly expanding populations; our drive to harvest forests for their wood, clear them for agriculture, slash through them with roads to aid commerce, burn down cover in times of war. All over Asia, tiger habitat has been encroached on, fragmented, destroyed. Hunting has taken its toll, of course, but loss of habitat has been most responsible for decimating tiger populations.

As wild habitat shrinks, tigers come into closer contact with people, provoking more conflict, inevitably leading to the death or capture of more tigers. Around the turn of the last century it was estimated that approximately 100,000 wild tigers roamed free across Asia. Today there are no more than 7,000 tigers living in the wild worldwide, perhaps as few as 5,000. And in most of the lands where they live, their numbers are declining.

"This film is about these animals and the effect that people have on them, as well the effect people have had on animals throughout history and all over the world."

— *ACTOR GUY PEARCE*

ING BROS AND **BARNU**
COMBINED SHOWS

CIRCUS A COMPLETE BIG TRAINED ANIMAL S

Tigers in Human Hands

Another notable fact about tigers is that they are highly adaptable. This means they can tolerate a wide range of habitats from the mangrove swamps of Burma to the snow-covered taiga of Siberia. It has also meant that they survive quite well—if not exactly thrive—in captivity. The fact that captive tigers breed readily may save the species from extinction, but ironically, means little for its future in nature. While some captive-bred species have been successfully reintroduced to the wild, this has not been the case for tigers—for a daunting list of reasons. Consequently, experts fear that in the not-too-distant future, zoos and game parks may be the only places where tigers survive at all.

Early records of tigers in captivity come from the Roman Empire, where rulers and commoners alike developed a taste for blood sports in the arena. Animals of all kinds as well as unfortunate humans were imported from the far corners of the empire and exhibited in the capital, reinforcing the Romans' sense of world dominion.

It's likely that even in ancient times, people of a scientific bent kept tigers captive, to observe or simply to enjoy their astounding beauty, grace, and power. There are records of early zoological collections in Egypt and in imperial China, Assyria, and Babylon. Alexander the Great collected animals on his campaigns and shipped them back to Greece. The Emperor Charlemagne had a zoo in the early ninth century, and explorer Hernán Cortes discovered great zoos kept by the Mexican royal families. During the Renaissance exotic animals were kept at the Tower of London, but they seldom survived long, as no one knew how to care for them.

ABOVE: Poster for a French circus with a Roman gladiatorial theme. LEFT: Poster for Ringling Bros. and Barnum & Bailey Big Trained Animal Show.

41

Around the mid-eighteenth century, organized zoos were established in European capitals in response to the scientific curiosity of the day as well as lingering imperial aspirations (the first was the Imperial Menagerie in Vienna's Schonbraun Palace). Little more than collections of cages in grand surroundings, these early zoos reflected vast ignorance about the needs of wild animals. Knowledge has expanded greatly in the few centuries since, and zoo conditions have improved immeasurably in many places, with modern zoos like those in San Diego, New York and Toronto housing animals in more or less natural surroundings.

Moral arguments can be made against keeping tigers (or any wild creature) captive; the issue is debated hotly in our era of rising consciousness of animals' rights. Those who operate and support zoos counter by arguing the need for scientific research that cannot be conducted in the wild, and more recently, for the importance of captive breeding of endangered species. The tiger is a poster child for the success of captive breeding—such success doesn't guarantee that tigers can continue to survive in their native habitats, but at least their genetic bases are being maintained.

The other venue where many people have gotten their first look at a tiger is the circus. Circuses are even more controversial than zoos these days: proponents of banning the use of wild animals as circus entertainment cite cases of neglect, serious abuse, or simply the cruel contrast between how creatures live in nature and the confinement, travel stress, and behavioral training they undergo in circus life.

ABOVE: Film still of the Cirque Zerbino tent and the circus set by the Mekong River. LEFT: Production drawing of one of Zerbino's trailer by Franc Schwartz.

Working to Keep Tigers Wild

Efforts to preserve tigers in the wild have gone on since the last few decades of the twentieth-century. They have become more coordinated in recent years, and international law prohibits trafficking in tiger parts. Yet poaching still thrives for lack of adequate enforcement, and the problems inherent in protecting habitat and keeping tigers and humans apart have intensified, if anything.

The makers of *Two Brothers*, naturally concerned with issues of tiger survival, have partnered with the World Wildlife Fund in France and the United States to raise public awareness and funds to protect tigers and their habitat.

Tigers are the top predators in some of the world's most diverse remaining forests, and successful tiger conservation can serve as an umbrella, protecting not just tigers but wild habitats and other species. WWF funds and equips anti-poaching patrols in key tiger forests, educates law enforcement about the importance of prosecuting poachers, conducts scientific research and monitoring of tiger populations, and works through public education to reduce demand for tiger parts by traditional medicine users.

Coincidentally, the filmmakers found themselves shooting right next door to a place where tigers still live in Cambodia. One of their principal locations was in the remote mountain province of Mondol Kiri, in the village of Putang.

Mondol Kiri teems with wildlife. It's the only part of Cambodia where a small population of wild tigers is proven to exist, along with other endangered species such as the Asian elephant, Asiatic black bear, leopard, and giant ibis. The Wildlife Conservation Society—the parent organization of the famed Bronx Zoo and another organization active in tiger conservation—has photographed wild tigers in the region and identified land suitable for a tiger reserve. WCS is coordinating conservation efforts there with Cambodia's Ministry of Agriculture, which recently established a protected conservation area of 1,400 square kilometers.

During a trip to the location, producer Jake Eberts paid a visit to the ranger station to see this work for himself. He reports, "We set out with a team of rangers to trek into the jungle to see where the camera traps were located. During the long hike through the undergrowth, we were able to see the tracks of wild elephant, durango, and most exciting of all, they showed us the fresh marks of tiger claws on some of the trees. It was an amazing experience—the kind of adventure that motivates me to make movies."

Annaud welcomes the opportunity to use the film to aid the efforts to establish the tiger reserve. "Conservation is very close to my heart. It is my hope that this film will raise the consciousness of audiences to the issue of protecting habitat for tigers and other creatures."

Jean-Jacques Annaud and a tiger cub greet Cambodia's Prince Norodom Ranariddh, who visited the Two Brothers *set.*

In *Two Brothers*, fate lands Kumal at a small itinerant circus, where the harsh trainer Saladin is opposed by the gentler circus owner, Zerbino. It's Kumal's bad luck that Saladin is the stronger character and gets his way.

It's sobering to realize that there are at least twice as many tigers living in captivity today as live in the wild. Wildlife experts are especially alarmed by a sharp rise in the number of private individuals who keep or breed tigers. For some people, visiting tigers in a zoo, or knowing they still roam the Asian forests, is not enough; they demand close-up contact to satisfy their tiger craving. They span the spectrum from Antoine Yates, who kept a 400-pound tiger named Ming in a housing project apartment in Harlem until discovered, to the owners of large ranches in Texas and California where scores of large carnivores roam.

People's motives for wanting to own tigers are mixed, but misguided at best. With few exceptions, they claim to be acting in the interest of conserving the species, though many display ignorance of the animal's basic biology and needs. It's patently obvious that an apartment is no place for a tiger, but even in a large, well-fenced landscape, maintaining tigers in a healthy and secure way is highly problematic. Baby tigers are flat-out adorable, as the *Two Brothers* crew can attest, but would-be tiger keepers don't stop to consider what happens when a 400-pound predator grows up—or they seriously overestimate their own ability to

ABOVE: *Zerbino (Vincent Scarito) and Saladin (Moussa Maaskri) at the Cirque Zerbino.* OPPOSITE: *Raoul (Freddie Highmore) falls asleep with his playmate Sangha.*

handle the situation. Some private owners' devotion to their tigers verges on mania; they insist it is worth any sacrifice even after they or their children have been attacked and injured.

In 2003, Congress passed, and President Bush signed, the Captive Wildlife Safety Act, which bans interstate trade in big cats for the pet trade. Humane groups hope this will be a first step curtailing the private ownership of tigers and other dangerous wild animals.

Annaud and the film deliver a strong message on this subject, through the plot line in which the little boy Raoul befriends the cub Sangha. "The Normandin family ends up having a young tiger as a pet, because their child falls in love with it," Annaud relates. "As we all do on the set. We all want to grab the baby tiger and play with it. Even after six months of seeing them every day, I can't resist. I have to cuddle them. So if you were to find a lost tiger cub in a temple, you would want to take it home. If you have a kid you will not be able to resist. Even if you know it's a mistake.

"But of course, after a few months the adorable creature Raoul cuddles with and sleeps with becomes a monster, and they must do something with it. In dramatizing Sangha's fate with this family, I'm showing the problem of what is to be done with that adorable baby when it becomes a grown-up animal and very dangerous."

After Sangha finally strikes back at the annoying dog that torments him, the family banishes him to a private zoo, where his innate shyness is warped into unpredictable ferocity. Later, after he and Kumal escape, the hunter McRory must explain to Raoul the hard reality of why Sangha must be killed. As a tiger accustomed to being around humans and never having learned to hunt natural prey, he is far more dangerous than a truly wild tiger. (This is one of the chief obstacles to reintroducing captive-bred tigers to the wild.)

"Tigers are extremely dangerous; they can kill you in a second," Annaud adds. "People often don't realize what they do."

A Place for Tigers?

"Exalted and denigrated and denigrated, admired and despised..." is how zoologist George Schaller describes humankind's attitude toward the great cats. Tigers have long haunted the landscapes of wild Asia and our mental landscapes, provoking many reactions—none of them mild. But now, as we face the likelihood that tigers may soon exist only behind protective barriers, what does it mean for our own species? Would the world lose some of its largeness and sense of potential? Would we humans lose one of the few remaining checks on our sense of invincibility and isolation from the rest of creation? Many believe so and, though the obstacles to maintaining viable tiger populations are enormous, are working desperately to keep tigers in wild places and keep places wild for them.

For now they survive only in far-flung outposts: national parks in India, a few reserves in far eastern Russia, the mountains of Sumatra, remote pockets of Indochina. A handful of wild tigers may still live in South China; no one knows for sure. Until recently, saving tigers has depended on isolated efforts by committed and influential individuals (like India's former prime minister Indira Gandhi), accidents of national policy (as when Stalin's Soviet regime expelled Chinese merchants from tiger country in the 1930s), and such pressure as international conservation groups could bring to bear.

Annaud and his production crew support this effort and made sure that the film project would contribute to the future of tigers in the wild. But his primary motives in making the film were more personal: a quest to bring people closer to tigers, not by seeking to possess them but by asking us to see the world through their eyes.

"I wanted to show that, from an animal's point of view, the reasons of man are very obscure," says Annaud. "Why (a tiger might wonder) would a man like McRory need to come to the jungle to find stones when there are already so many around his den, his home? Likewise, from a tiger's viewpoint all the political maneuvers in the story are incomprehensible. The governor wants a road, which makes no sense to the tiger and yet is going to affect the tiger's life.

"The life of animals is always troubled by human activity, more than we realize. If you're a tiger in Cambodia today, your biggest problem is that Chinese furniture makers love the hardwood from the Cambodian forest. On one level that can be an innocent desire: a hard-working man in China wants to make his wife happy by giving her a nice piece of furniture for their wedding anniversary. But he's not helping the tigers. In showing the tiger's point of view, I can hope that people will start to see things in a different way. Perhaps that man would not buy the piece of furniture if he knows that getting the wood is going to kill ten families of tigers.

"When *The Bear* came out, there was a very amusing drawing in the *New Yorker*," Annaud recalls. "It showed a group of moviegoers, all bears, coming out of a movie called *The Salmon*, and they were saying: 'We didn't know that salmon hated us.' In any case, by changing the perspective I am trying to enable us humans to see ourselves from another point of view. To what we do in light of the tragedy it creates in the lives of my two heroes."

> Tigers, panthers, jaguars, lions, etc. Whence comes the emotion that the sight of all that produces in me? From the fact that I am lifted out of the everyday thoughts that make up all my world, out of my street which is my universe. How necessary it is to rouse oneself from time to time, to stick one's head outdoors, to read something of the creation which has nothing in common with our cities or the works of men!
>
> — PAINTER EUGÈNE DELACROIX, 1847

Conjuring Colonial Indochina

Seeking the milieu for his tale of two tigers,

Jean-Jacques Annaud's personal compass pulled him back to the place that had made such a profound impact on him years earlier: the breathtaking temples of Angkor, set amid the timeless beauty of the Indochinese forest near the city of Siem Reap.

"When I first visited the temple complex in 1989, I was so excited," the director recalls. "I came with just one roll of film, and after two minutes it was gone. When I went back to the city to get more, I could find only 16 rolls, and I used it all up in a few hours. I just could not stop.

"Cambodia had everything I was looking for to make *Two Brothers*," he continues. "The splendor of the temples together with the serenity and beauty of the landscape. It also invoked the nostalgia of the colonial period, the mystery of the forest, and above all, the soul of the people."

During his writing phase, Annaud pored over research materials about early twentieth-century Southeast Asia. "I found marvelous photographs, watercolors, models, and paintings that inspired my story. In particular, there was an engraving from around 1880 that I loved. It shows some beautiful, romantic temples all tangled in vegetation, and in the lefthand corner there is a small tiger. This image stayed in my mind and probably generated the first vision for the film."

Two years before filming began, Annaud went back to Cambodia to see if it matched his early impressions: "to find out whether it had been too cleaned up by tourism, with big hotels next to the ruins. Fortunately, things had not changed much. It was still marvelous and romantic, the way I'd seen it. Cambodia remains a very authentic, almost medieval Asia in many ways. The Asia you dream of, with beautiful rice fields, ox carts in the countryside."

ABOVE: Le Temple de la Jungle, ink-and-watercolor illustration by Jean Despujols. Indochina Collection, Meadows Museum of Art, Centenary College of Louisiana. LEFT: Angkor, Baion Ruins, illustration from Atlas du voyage d'exploration en Indochine, 1866-68, *by Doudart de Lagree, published by French School (19th century) Bibliotheque des Arts Decoratifs, Paris, France. OPPOSITE: Tiger cubs nestle in the lap of a Buddha created for the set.*

"Cambodia remains a very authentic, almost medieval Asia in many ways. The Asia you dream of, with beautiful rice fields, ox carts in the countryside."

—*JEAN-JACQUES ANNAUD*

Pre-production began in 2001 when Annaud and line producer Xavier Castano embarked on extensive location scouting. Although they visited other locations including Australia and Thailand, Cambodia was always the first choice—especially after it became apparent that they could do virtually everything within a two-hour radius of Siem Reap.

"Jean-Jacques personally chose all the locations," explains producer Jake Eberts. "Who would not be fascinated by Angkor and the many other remarkable temples of Cambodia?"

Castano, who had worked closely with Annaud on *The Bear* 15 years earlier, was the director's indispensable lieutenant both in pre-production and during the shoot. This veteran of French cinema had a long résumé as an assistant or second unit director (*Jean de Florette, Manon of the Spring*) and production manager (*Valmont*). Since working on *The Bear*, he had executive produced *Belle Maman* and taken the helm as director on *Veraz* in 1991. Castano put his own directing ambitions on hold, however, to help his old friend on this challenging shoot. "We are very close, and what we do together is always something we both like. The direction and the production go very much together. He told me that we needed to travel to Cambodia together to see if we have the same feeling about the country and the story."

"Xavier had the immense responsibility of organizing the whole effort in Cambodia: making contact with the local authorities, getting permissions, building roads, putting the crew together," says Annaud. "I am so grateful to him—he's a very good friend and a wonderful worker."

Their scouting journeys and preliminary budgeting made it clear to Annaud and Castano that filming this script called for a wide range of scenic resources. In addition to shooting in half a dozen locations around Cambodia, some scenes (both exteriors and interiors) would be filmed in Thailand, and additional interior shots would be completed at a studio in Paris.

Another key team member in bringing the film's physical world to life was production designer Pierre Queffelean, heading up the art department. *Two Brothers* was Queffelean's first assignment at this level, though he had been chief assistant to Annaud's favorite production designer, At Hoang, on *Seven Years in Tibet*.

"At the time I needed to move forward, At Hoang was having health problems, and we knew this would be a difficult shoot with the heat and dust and a lot of travel," Annaud explains. "Rather than bring in someone unknown, I gave the job to Pierre, who I knew was very creative. I saw how good he was during *Seven Years in Tibet*—he was responsible for a lot of sets and it was clear he had excellent taste. He went on the scouting trip with us, and I felt right from the beginning that he was terrific."

"We had three weeks of location scouting with Jean-Jacques," says Queffelean. "He took a lot of pictures, which helped us to develop our designs. Then we made detailed drawings to get the right Cambodian atmosphere."

Annaud always relies on providing his creative team with extensive source materials—in this case, literally hundreds of images from his research and from the location scout. Then he commissions detailed renderings of his sets. "Because I wanted people to understand what I wanted, I made notes, I sent documentation. And I hold lots of meetings. Because if it doesn't look the way I want it, I can't shoot. I don't even know where to put my camera."

But after scouting Angkor, Annaud had a very good idea of his future camera angles. He could virtually see the tiger cubs in a scene from the script, playing in the rocky landscape around the temples. After visiting one vivid bas-relief, he recalls the eerie feeling of having written about this image before ever having seen it.

*THESE PAGES: Jean-Jacques Annaud and his photos
of scouting the temples for locations in 2001.*

Temples in the Jungle

"We were shooting in one of the Seven Wonders of the World, so we had to take every precaution to make sure that there was no damage to the location." Jean-Jacques Annaud thus sums up one of the central challenges in making *Two Brothers*.

No one who visits Angkor fails to understand why this vast complex of temples was deemed one of the original Seven Wonders. The ruined capital of the Khmer Empire, built from around 900–1400 A.D.,

sprawls over a landscape of 120 square miles, larger than Greater London; it encompasses more than 100 monuments including two dozen major temples. Angkor Wat, the largest and best known, covers an area of two square kilometers alone. Contemporary with Notre Dame in Paris, it is the largest religious site in the world, its volume of stone equaling that of Egypt's Great Pyramid.

These stupendous ruins are the legacy of a powerful, creative people and the god-kings they memorialized in stone. The Khmer rulers built their great temples to link the human and divine in life and unite them in death. The first important king, Jayavarman II, in 802 A.D. established a capital close to the great lake of Tonle Sap, beginning the Khmers' rise to power. Jayavarman was proclaimed a "universal monarch" in the cult of the *deva-raj*— an Indian concept of divine kingship. The Khmer used it to assert their claim to surrounding lands against rivals such as the empire of Java to the south. By this time, the early civilizations of Southeast Asia had been exposed for several centuries to the highly developed culture of India, and the art and architecture that emerged at Angkor was basically a local refinement of Indian models.

For the next six centuries the Khmers dominated mainland Southeast Asia. By the twelfth century, Angkor's influence extended south to the Mekong delta in present-day Vietnam, north into Laos, and west over much of what is now Thailand. Jayavarman II's successors built *barays*, man-made lakes adjacent to the temples, which fed a complex network of irrigation channels. This sophisticated system of agricultural hydraulics enabled the Khmers to produce two or three harvests a year and thus to build their empire.

From this solid economic base, Indravarman I began the tradition of temple building. It reached its artistic height under Suryavarman II, who conceived Angkor Wat and whose battles are celebrated on its bas-reliefs, and Jayavarman VII, who constructed the city of Angkor Thom. "It is grander than anything left us by Greece and Rome," wrote Henri Mouhot, the French explorer who rediscovered Ankgor, in his diary. Key elements of the temples include galleries, courtyards, and massive terraces surrounding multiple towers, or pyramidal temple-mounts—the symbolic home of the god-king, often bearing his likeness. Some sites also contained residential palaces, government buildings, and moats or canals traversed by pillared causeways.

"We were shooting in one of the Seven Wonders of the World, so we had to take every precaution to make sure that there was no damage to the location."

—JEAN-JACQUES ANNAUD

ABOVE: *Aerial view of Angkor Wat, the largest of the Khmer empire sites.* OPPOSITE: *Production drawings of the temple sets by Franc Schwartz.*

All the buildings are incredibly rich in sculptural ornament. There are countless free-standing sculptures, but the pinnacle of Khmer artistry is the fabulously ornate bas-reliefs that cover thousands of feet of wall space. These impeccably crafted carvings, more delicately proportioned than their Indian prototypes, illustrate scenes from the legends of Vishnu and Krishna, or historical events from the lives of kings. Mythical animals, too, cavort on some reliefs: royal elephants, divine serpents, monkey gods, half-bird/half-human creatures—and of course, tigers.

Explorers, Restorers, and Tomb Raiders

Rival kingdoms that strove for power with the Khmer empire included those of Annam and Champa (both more or less in what is now Vietnam) and the Thai, who captured Angkor in 1431. After this, the capital was moved to Phnom Penh, and though Angkor was briefly restored as a royal city in the 1570s, most of the temples were abandoned to the surrounding forest.

By the nineteenth century, when France became the dominant colonial power in this part of Asia, Angkor's stonework was weathered and melting under the patient onslaught of tree roots, liana vines, monsoon, and sun. Forest creatures—tigers, monkeys, snakes, and birds—roamed the galleries and stalked atop the boundary walls. This was the scene when, in 1861, a French botanist named Henri Mouhot, in the course of a four-year expedition to study Indochina's plant life, hacked his way through the forest to Angkor, where he spent three weeks studying the temples and falling under their spell. Mouhot did not survive his Asian sojourn, but his journals—published posthumously in 1864 as *Travels in Siam, Cambodia and Laos*—evoked Angkor's wonders so vividly that the romance of the ruined city seized the Western imagination, where it still holds a firm grip.

The reports of Mouhot and others had potent and contradictory effects. On the positive side, as archeologists and art historians recognized the enormous importance of Angkor, the French government undertook an intensive research and restoration program. Begun in 1908, it continued on and off until interrupted by the Vietnam war and Cambodian civil unrest in the 1960s through 1980s.

After peace was restored in 1991, aid from developed nations poured in to help save Angkor. France, India, Germany, and Japan all sent teams and money; later, the U.S.-based World Monuments Fund joined the effort. The Cambodian agency APSARA, which oversees the work, has sometimes been hard-pressed to coordinate all the projects and keep peace among experts with different ideas about how restoration should be done. Some early projects, for example, used corrosive chemicals that damaged and blurred the carvings. A UNESCO-

OPPOSITE: Detail of Emile Gsell's glass-plate photograph of the temple of Bayon, c. 1866 or 1873. Réunion des Musées Nationaux/ Art Resource, NY.

"At Ongcor [Ankgor], there are . . . ruins of such grandeur . . . that, at the first view, one is filled with profound admiration, and cannot but ask what has become of this powerful race, so civilized, so enlightened, the authors of these gigantic works?"

—HENRI MOUHOT, 1861

sponsored master plan was shelved some years back, but an international committee now works to foster communication among the teams, and Cambodians are being trained to replace the native archaeologists, architects, and craftsmen who died during the Khmer Rouge reign of terror.

Most of the major temples, including Angkor Wat, Angkor Thom, and Banteay Srei, have been extensively restored. Two temples, however, have been largely left as they were discovered in the late 1800s, as jungle-choked ruins. Ta Prohm and Preah Khan are extremely popular with some visitors for exactly this reason; in this wildly romantic setting, on a quiet day, one can almost imagine being the first outsider to stumble on their crumbling glories.

While restoration and preservation have been the official program at Angkor for nearly a century, with tourism not far behind, those early reports of its splendor provoked a darker reaction. Driven by greed and desire, fortune hunters and collectors journeyed to the land of the Khmers to carry away treasures, just as the film depicts. Understandably, they were aided and abetted by local people, to whom the remains of their ancestors' cities often meant less than the money they could earn for their families.

Temple raiders were not always sleazy characters by any means. One of the first and most notorious cases of looting took place at Banteay Srei in 1923, when the young André Malraux pulled off a major heist, haul-

Before him lay a chaos of fallen stones . . . it looked like a mason's yard invaded by the jungle. Here were lengths of wall in slabs of purple sandstone, some carved and others plain, all plumed with pendent ferns. Some bore a red patina, the aftermath of fire. Facing him he saw some bas-reliefs of the best period, marked by Indian influences—he was now close up to them—but very beautiful work; they were grouped round an old shrine, half hidden now behind a breastwork of fallen stones. It cost him an effort to take his eyes off them.

—ANDRÉ MALRAUX, *THE ROYAL WAY*

ing away a large bas-relief from the temple to sell. Colonial authorities tracked him down, confiscated the sculptures and returned them to the site, and put France's future Minister of Culture on trial. Malraux's novel *The Royal Way* (1930) was closely based on the incident.

Looting remains a problem in some of the more isolated sites, as sculptures can fetch hundreds of thousands of dollars in the underground collectors' market. But most Cambodians now recognize that their best chance for prosperity may lie with the tourists who flock to Angkor from around the world. And their government does its best to keep the all-important restoration work moving forward. As a 1993 UNESCO publication stated, the site's importance "makes its long-term preservation both a national desire and a symbol of the reconciliation and rehabilitation of Cambodian society."

Cinema Amid the Ruins

While Annaud did not want to set *Two Brothers* in any specific place or time period, he imagined the story taking place soon after the temples were rediscovered. Production designer Pierre Queffelean notes, "Creating the right atmosphere was more important than the precise period. Today many of the temples have been cleared, and the stones are exposed, so we had to re-create the overgrown environment of the beginning of the century."

The temple of Ta Prohm was the logical place to start, and it became the primary set for the tigers' jungle sanctuary. Even the minimal restoration that has occurred here made the setting too tidy, so the production crew had to "unrestore" it—doing nothing to change the monument itself but bringing in more vegetation, adding fallen or broken statuary made by the art department, obscuring the neat footpaths, and so on.

"The first location we shot in was Ta Prohm, one of the most beautiful temples in Angkor," Queffelean notes. Built in 1186 by Jayavarman VII, Ta Prohm has been invaded by the huge roots of strangler fig trees. Lead greensman Thierry Lemaire did "an enormous amount of work to enhance the vegetation, to cover these sublime ruins with a mix of real vines and fake ones in polystyrene. We added about 25,000 plants to the set," says Queffelean.

While most of the exterior shots of the tigers' sanctuary were done at Ta Prohm, requirements for lighting, tiger handling, and other action required using a set for interior shots. Late in the shoot, the whole production moved to Bangkok, where a number of sets were constructed in a huge stadium. Here Queffelan designed and art director Steve Spence built a replica of the interior of the Ta Prohm temple, which enabled Annaud to do a traveling shot all the way along the corridor.

Although the set was mostly made of polystyrene, it was necessary to reinforce the base with

ABOVE: Shooting at the temple set that was re-created in a stadium in Bangkok. OPPOSITE: During his temple raid in the film, Aidan blasts a huge statue loose, and his crew carries it away (overleaf).

> "The temple fights a slow battle with nature. The integration of architecture and vegetation provided an incredible backdrop for the scenes with the tigers."
>
> —PRODUCTION DESIGNER PIERRE QUEFFELEAN

Taking Care of Ta Prohm

Before the production could even contemplate doing an elaborate shoot at Ta Prohm, they had to get official permission to take over the site for several weeks, during which time it would be closed to the public. It fell to Xavier Castano to negotiate this delicate request with APSARA. "It wasn't easy because they had had a bad experience with another film company recently.

"The temples of Angkor are some of the most popular tourist attractions in the world," Castano continues. "This meant that all the tour operators had to be informed months in advance that certain temples would be closed and precisely when. We worked very closely with APSARA, the Authority for the Protection and Management of Angkor and the Region of Siem Reap, which is in charge of research, protection, and conservation of cultural heritage, as well as urban and tourist development. We came to enjoy a really wonderful relationship with them."

Protecting the ancient stone walkways, bridges, and terraces from the crew's traffic was a high priority. Castano explains, "First the surfaces were covered with sand, and then wood was placed on top so that a footbridge was created for the crew to access the sets without ever touching the stones."

Although shooting in the actual temples posed huge logistical problems, there was never any question about whether it was worthwhile. "If we had to re-create it in studios or somewhere else, it would have been a gigantic amount of work," says Queffelean. "And you could never truly reproduce this extraordinary atmosphere."

plaster and concrete. Says Queffelean, "In general, we had to think about strong sets, strong enough for the tigers to lean on the walls or scratch them, and to walk on firm surfaces. A lot of things made with cement and glue, which are very heavy decoration elements." However, "it's not just to be strong enough to hold the tigers," explains Spence. "Thierry Le Portier told me it is important that it feels real under the tigers' feet, or they get nervous."

The major difference between the stadium set and Ta Prohm is that the set required a greater concentration of detail. Features from all parts of the temple were reduced to a much smaller area. Most of the statues for the set were made in Cambodia of concrete, modeled on originals in the National Museum in Phnom Penh. "We met the museum director, who authorized us to make direct copies of the originals," explains Queffelean. "Aesthetically

they are perfect. The big Buddha, though, we made in Thailand out of polystyrene, because concrete would have been too heavy. The frieze of elephants on the wall of the arena was done the same way."

Annaud wanted a subtle effect for the great smiling Buddha statue that is blasted out of its place by McRory's raiders. Steve Spence notes, "Jean-Jacques wanted to give the impression that over the years the water running over the statue had formed a rivulet, which looked like the Buddha had a tear falling from his eye."

The crew also created a wall relief depicting the story of a tiger hunt. Queffelean made drawings based on details from Ta Prohm and other temples, and the resulting design was then carved into polystyrene. Three sculptors constructed the wall in three sections. Each section took about two weeks. Then painters applied as many as 20 layers of paint to the final design.

By the Sacred River

Although the temples near Angkor were easily accessible from Siem Reap, other locations were not as simple to get to. The scenes where the tigers relax by a riverbank, seen both at the beginning and the end of the film, were shot at Kbal Spean, an extraordinary site 60 kilometers from Siem Reap. It can only be reached after a 30-minute hike up a mountain trail, and most of the equipment had to be airlifted in by helicopter. Other supplies were carried by porters or taken in on horseback.

Kbal Spean is known as the "River of a Thousand Lingas" because of the amazing carvings inscribed in the riverbed rock and flanking boulders. These images from the eleventh century display a gallery of gods and celestial beings from Indian and Khmer mythology. Some of the carvings are submerged by river waters, others are open to the elements, and a few have been chipped away by thieves. In one small area there are thousands of sculpted *lingas*, or phallic images, and

ABOVE: Detail of the big Buddha with "tear track."
OPPOSITE: A tiger emerges from a doorway at Ta Prohm.

a large underwater rendering of a *yoni* (womb). The fast-running waters of Kbal Spean are said to be blessed with fertility as they pass over the sacred *lingas*, then flow down the mountain to the fields of Angkor.

Producer Jake Eberts calls Kbal Spean "one of my favorite sites in the world. This is truly one of the most spiritual places on the planet—to see that location alone is worth the price of a visit to Cambodia."

Line producer Xavier Castano, faced with the day-to-day reality of shooting in this inaccessible spot, had a somewhat different reaction. "When I first saw Kbal Spean, I told Jean-Jacques that we should look for another river—one very close to the road—and have our art department create the carvings." So they looked at various rivers in Cambodia and Thailand, but couldn't find anything that worked. "I am a very strange producer," Castano admits. "Jean-Jacques knows that I couldn't sell a bad idea, even if it was my idea. You could never create what you feel in Kbal Spean, even if you have a great production designer. I knew early on that we would end up there."

Once filming in the Siem Reap area was complete, the production traveled to Phnom Penh, Cambodia's capital, to shoot a huge market scene in the center of the city. "Shooting in Phnom Penh was very complicated," says Castano. "The square we chose for the location housed the main post office and a bank. We had to transform the bank into a jail."

Pierre Queffelean describes some of the difficulties involved in transforming a piece of present-day Phnom Penh back to colonial times. "To create the market in the middle of the plaza, we had to close down all traffic—

but we couldn't do that for long, as it's a busy intersection. We had to cover the facades of many buildings, dealing with all the merchants one by one. The buildings were well-maintained when it was a French colony, but now some of the facades are quite damaged and didn't match the time period, so we had to restore them."

Other locations around Phnom Penh included Pook, where the scene of the tigress chasing the truck was shot, and Kampong Cham, a town upriver from the capital, where another scene was shot using a spectacular, half-mile-long bamboo bridge. A six-hour riverboat journey up the Mekong took the crew to the next location, Kratie, for the rafting scene. From there, the crew drove for eight hours through the jungle on dirt roads to Putang, a village in the remote mountain province of Mondol Kiri, where the production settled into a small tent city for several weeks of shooting. (See "The Journey Is the Reward.")

LEFT: Filming a scene on the bamboo bridge near Kampong Cham, on the Mekong. OPPOSITE: The extraordinary carvings in the Kbal Spean riverbed are visible through the water.

What They Wore

In costuming, as with the other visual components of *Two Brothers*, Jean-Jacques Annaud was seeking not to reconstitute a precise period but to evoke the mood and spirit of Southeast Asian colonial society, circa early 1900s. Costume designer Pierre-Yves Gayraud, whose credits include work on *The Bourne Identity, La Guerre à Paris, Imago, Total Eclipse,* and *Indochine,* says, "For Jean-Jacques it's not a period movie, but we have to find the spirit of the period. We had freedom to be creative. The important thing was that the costumes for each principal felt very personal, realistic, true to the character."

Other than a few specialized costumes rented in England, Gayraud's team made all the costumes on site in Cambodia, using fabrics found there and in Bangkok and Paris. He brought a team of seven costumers with him from France and hired nearly 50 Cambodian workers to assist in making costumes for the principals and extras—including all 400 extras in the arena scene. They ranged from women's fashions of the day to military uniforms, McRory's safari garb, and the traditional dress of ordinary and high-ranking Indochinese. Dying fabrics and embroidering elaborate decoration were among the tasks carried out in the Phnom Penh costume shop.

Gayraud has high praise for his crew: "Even though most of our Cambodian crew were doing this kind of work for the first

THESE PAGES: Costume drawings of Aidan's safari garb and Indochinese characters: a servant, an elephant driver, and a gardener, along with costume details, by Pierre-Yves Gayraud and Gael Roger.

time, they did a very good job. The main thing was taking the time to explain exactly what we wanted."

On top of the need to stay close to the shooting unit for fittings, cleanings, repairs, and so on, Gayraud prefers to do his work on site whenever possible, making decisions based on the local conditions. "I prefer to wait until the last moment to decide exactly the right weight for fabrics, to see how they will react to sweat and dust and so on. And I look at the set to get ideas.

"Jean-Jacques wants us to find whatever will create the reality for this picture—the dust or humidity, whatever. In the studio, you would have to put water on the clothes to recreate this atmosphere."

Per usual practice, the costumers made multiples of certain costumes that would see heavy or repeated use. Maintaining continuity is another challenge when a costume sports mud or bloodstains and must look the same from shot to shot. "We have some doubles for hunting and for stunts, for example, when characters are physically interacting with the tiger," notes Gayraud. "And because Guy Pearce wears the same costume many times, I think we had seven copies of that one. And we did a lot of cleaning!"

From Circus to Palace to Arena

After leaving Mondol Kiri, the company moved to Bangkok, which offered a variety of resources that served the production's needs. Several scenes required very complicated work with the tigers, and Annaud wanted all the comforts of a studio for the tigers so they would be alert and could concentrate on their acting. So in an air-conditioned football stadium outside the city, the crew constructed many of the film's interior sets—for example, the interior corridor of Ta Prohm temple described earlier. Here too, they created the Prince's gorgeously decorated underground menagerie. "For this we made a beautiful temple-style decoration in low relief," says Pierre Queffelean, "with a projection of a tiger's shadow."

Although the exterior shots of the small-time Circus Zerbino, where Kumal grows up to be a performing tiger, were shot in Kampong Cham, the evocative interiors were filmed in the studio (this time back in Paris).

Again, this was partly so that the tigers could focus on their work in these scenes: including subtle behavioral acting in depicting the relationship between Kumal and the old circus tiger.

Annaud's loving attention to detail shows especially in these sets, which were informed by his reading and inspired by other filmmakers who have explored the circus world. "I adore the images of circus from Fellini's movies. The circus was a key inspiration for him, for films like *The Clowns* and *La Strada.*"

Perhaps the most rewarding discovery in Bangkok was a theme park outside the city called Muang Boran. Here the production found full-sized replicas of some of Thailand's most beautiful temples, models of Thai houses, and beautiful gardens with lakes and streams full of water lilies. The interiors of one of the palace replicas became the set for the Prince's residence in the story. "These interiors were pretty amazing," notes Queffelean. "Jean-Jacques and I thought they were perfect for the Prince's palace, full of details, molding, and inlaid walls with precious stones. Philippe Turlure, our set decorator, dressed the set by adding things like pillars and furniture."

The park-like setting of Muang Boran turned out to be the ideal location for the film's climactic scene, in which the brother tigers are pitted against each other like gladiators in an arena—an event that draws hundreds of spectators. The featured actors and 400 extras employed in the scene (all in period costume) strolled toward their destination through lush gardens with bridges arching over a lake. The arena itself was constructed from scratch in a style designed to match the backdrop of palaces and gardens, a fantastical setting that suited the fairy-tale theme.

ABOVE: His Excellency (Oanh Nguyen) and Paulette (Stéphanie Legarde) pose with a tiger skin in the palace interior. OPPOSITE: Sangha is brought to his new home in the Prince's underground menagerie, with wall detail created by the art department.

"Le Cirque ZERBINO"

PRECEDING PAGES: *The raft set created for Aidan (Guy Pearce) and Nai-Rea's (Mai Anh Le) river journey.* THIS PAGE, CLOCKWISE FROM TOP: *Drawing for the Cirque Zerbino by At Hoang. Drawings by Franc Schwartz of the village chief's house and the town market square, with a unit photo of Annaud and his team in the marketplace.* OPPOSITE, TOP: *Normandin (Jean-Claude Dreyfus) shows off his road model to local dignitaries at the governor's house.* OPPOSITE, BOTTOM: *Annaud directs a scene from His Excellency's box at the arena.*

Says Annaud, "The little arena we built was inspired by pictures of arenas from many fascinating old books about animal fighting. From those documents to the final set was an evolution, of course."

From Bangkok, the production moved to Paris to finish principal photography at Arpejon Studios. Besides the circus, a number of interior scenes were shot here, including the residence of Governor Normandin, where Sangha lives for a brief blissful time with Normandin's young son, Raoul. For this exterior, Annaud had used an original colonial house in Cambodia, "but we couldn't find a colonial interior that looked like what Jean-Jacques wanted," says Queffelean.

Complicating the set needs for chez Normandin, the crew had to stage a complicated chase scene, where the family's yapping little dog pursues Sangha through the house, wreaking havoc as they go. "We needed a place where we could move the walls around easily. That's why we ended up doing it in the studio," Queffelean explains. Director of photography Jean-Marie Dreujou also had a special challenge in this scene: The camera had to be placed very low to the ground to capture the racing animals at their level. He and Queffelean solved the problem by adding a special ceiling and lighting the scene from the outside.

The Characters

"**The stars are the tigers,**" declares Jean-Jacques Annaud. With that kind of movie premise, casting actors and building character portrayals pose different challenges than for most films. Still, *Two Brothers* is quite different from *The Bear*, in which the focus was almost entirely on the animals and there was almost no spoken dialogue. Here, telling the story required some exposition through dialogue, and Annaud was interested in presenting human viewpoints as well: that of the hunter Aidan McRory, whose life and thinking are changed by his encounters with the tigers; of the child Raoul, whose response to the cub Sangha is pure enchantment; of the jaded circus folk; and of the tiger-phobic natives.

In scriptwriting, Annaud and Alain Godard carefully balanced their ingredients so that the human element would season the plot and move along the action where needed—while always keeping the fate of Kumal and Sangha foremost in our minds. Whereas most films emphasize the complex and multi-layered personalities of the human characters, and animals function merely as appendages to the humans, in this film the people are important only to the extent that they affect the tigers. Fascinated by "the buffoonery and quirky characters of the colonial world," Annaud and Godard deliberately created two-dimensional, human characters, almost caricatures, to serve as counterpoint to the much more substantial and compelling personalities of the tigers. They also lend some comic flavor to this essentially serious story.

Annaud set out to assemble an eclectic mix of actors for *Two Brothers*. "I just wanted great actors that can perform well. It's a relief when you don't necessarily have to go with stars but can freely cast people because you trust their talent and feel they are right for the part.

"What I really enjoy is putting people from different backgrounds together on the same set—a famous film star, beginners, children, tigers, circus performers, theater actors who have never acted in front of a camera before. They all help each other; they all try to learn from each other, impress each other.

"Most of the cast are trained actors," he notes. "They've done movies before; they know each other. There's no surprise. But when you put a child or an animal in the middle of all this, it's different. It's unpredictable because the ingredients are fresh and new. If you cook with the same ingredients all the time, the dish will have a familiar flavor. If you go with a little more invention, it's more risky for the cook but it tastes better."

RIGHT: *Annaud talks with Guy Pearce and Philippine Leroy-Beaulieu about a scene.*

73

Kumal

Of the two brothers, Kumal is the more assertive and courageous—at least at the start of the movie. Says Jean-Jacques Annaud, "He is the dominant one of the pair." After being captured by McRory, though, he winds up in the Circus Zerbino as the heir apparent to an old performing tiger that's on his last legs. Kumal shows too much spirit to suit the bad trainer Saladin, but after the tiger is finally "tamed" he performs his tricks listlessly "with no desire for life and no guts," says Annaud. That is, until he is reunited with brother Sangha and they escape together.

Eliciting comments from Kumal and Sangha about their moviemaking experience was complicated by the fact that each was played by nine different tigers, of different ages and abilities. We imagined that they might have said something like what follows, which is based on the tigers' actual performances and interviews with their trainers.

Kumal: "I did a lot of work with our lead human actor, Guy Pearce. He was okay, and I think he really liked us tigers. At first he didn't know how to handle us and he would hold me the wrong way, so I got scared and angry and tried to climb on top of him. I might even have bit him a little once. But our trainer Thierry showed him how to do it the right way, and he learned pretty quickly. I mean, I was just a baby tiger—I do whatever I feel like, and the humans have to deal with it. Anyway, Guy was nice. He used to come see us after the filming when he didn't have to.

"When I had to fight my brother Sangha in the arena, I wasn't too interested at first because the tiger who played Sangha, he's sort of my buddy. But we're competitive, too; we're both male tigers and we can't be in the same place together for very long without each of us wanting to be the boss. So we start kind of play-fighting, and when it got too serious, Thierry would come in and break us up. But I guess they got what they wanted on film. In the end, we make up anyway.

"This is the first movie I've done, but maybe not the last. Because Thierry says he's going to keep all of the tigers who worked on this movie, and he does a lot of films with his animals. So who knows?"

Sangha

Sangha, the more timid of the brothers, also goes through a character evolution, but in a much different way than Kumal. "This brother started in life as the dominated one," says Annaud, "but becomes a very aggressive, fighting tiger." Sangha is left orphaned when his mother is apparently killed in a tiger hunt, and is taken home by the Normandin family after their son Raoul finds him hiding in a burrow. But then . . . we'll let Sangha tell it himself.

Sangha: "Well, my character gets in trouble as I'm growing up because this stupid dog keeps chasing me around the house where I am living. One day I just got fed up with it and did what tigers do . . . I guess it wasn't a good idea because all the humans were really upset. Then they sent me away."

The Normandins ship Sangha off to a private menagerie owned by the local Prince whose father kept animals to fight in public spectacles. The zookeeper recognizes that Sangha is a good candidate, because his fear can easily be turned into aggression. The Prince decides to stage a fight to show how tough they both are, if he can find another tiger to do battle. That sets the stage for the film's climax and the brothers' reunion.

Sangha: "It's sometimes hard to tell Kumal and me apart. But later in the movie I have to wear this big collar all crusted with jewels that the Prince gave me, so you know who I am right away.

"Right before that was the scary fire scene. We tigers don't mind the heat so much; it's the light and movement that makes us nervous. And the noise: When the whole forest was burning, it sounded like thunder. Our trainers were there to make sure nothing happened to us, but still . . . the only way we could get out was through the fire. I was afraid and wouldn't go, but Kumal had learned to jump through flaming hoops in the circus. He showed me how to jump through it without getting hurt. Then we got to go lie in the river and cool off.

"Acting is fun sometimes and kind of annoying sometimes. The people would get us to perform by doing crazy things—like opening and shutting an umbrella really fast or making sudden loud noises. You should have seen our director, the famous Monsieur Annaud, trying to get us to do something: jumping around like a madman and blowing a whistle and banging on a metal box. He didn't look very dignified."

Aidan McRory GUY PEARCE

"Aidan is the key human character," explains Annaud, "possibly the only character who finally understands the point of view of the animal." Of his lead actor, Guy Pearce, he says, "I think he's perfect for the part, and I knew it would be a difficult part for an actor. Guy knew very well that the tigers are the stars. The first time we met I knew he was the right person. The way he talked about the script, the way he talked about animals. He has an immense sensitivity to living creatures."

Both script and animals persuaded Pearce to take on the role. "When I read the script, I'd just been on a holiday in Cambodia. It was the first script I'd ever seen that had pictures in it, the temples and so on, and I'd

be saying, 'We've just been there, and there.' That was one thing that made me sit up and take notice. But what most attracted me was the fact that I would be working with tigers.

"Because it was very much about the effect people have on animals rather than the people's own importance, I felt like I could slip into this movie and not feel there was a great deal of pressure on me. I liked the idea that it works in opposition to what you're normally doing as an actor. The animals just do what they want, and we have to work around that."

Pearce is unlikely to escape the spotlight even in this film where he claims a secondary role, after his compelling performance in the suspense thriller *Memento*. He had previously garnered praise for his role as detective Ed Exley in Curtis Hanson's award-winning film noir drama *LA Confidential*. His work in the latter brought Pearce a SAG Award nomination, shared with his fellow cast members. He has also starred in the Australian film *The Hard Word*, the retelling of H.G Wells's classic *The Time Machine*, and in Kevin Reynolds's swashbuckling drama *The Count of Monte Cristo*. Pearce first gained international attention when he starred as a young drag performer in *Priscilla, Queen of the Desert*. His other recent film credits include *Till Human Voices Wake Us* and William Friedkin's military drama *Rules of Engagement*.

As Annaud describes his character in *Two Brothers*, "Aidan is a former hunter who is now hunting statues in the forest. He is at a moment of his life where, without really knowing it, he's fed up with the killing. His encounter with the tigers drives the whole story and changes his life completely."

ABOVE AND OPPOSITE: Guy Pearce with Mai Anh Le (Nai-Rea) and with one of his tiger friends.

"I was astounded every day just to be around these animals. Just their physical nature was overwhelming—even though the cubs are small, they're very heavy and strong, and they've got such deep voices even at that stage."

—GUY PEARCE

"His character is somewhat based on hunting guides I've met," the director adds. "people who come to hate their work, finding animals for rich people to shoot. Guy and I discussed this idea, for example, in playing the scene of the tiger hunt."

Working with the tigers—especially the young cubs—was everything Pearce imagined it might be and more. "I'm a big cat fan anyway; I've had cats all my life. I'm not suggesting that domestic cats are anything like tigers, but instinctively I felt very at home with the cubs. I found it easy understand how they were feeling most of the time: when they were not happy, when they were tired and wanted to stop.

"It was a completely amazing experience. I was astounded every day just to be around these animals. There's something unquestioning about them, and there's no hidden agenda. Just their physical nature was overwhelming—even though the cubs are small, they're very heavy and strong, and they've got such deep voices even at that stage.

"I loved it when they started to think I was their mother and follow me around. Once that moment occurs, when it decides you're the one that is going to take care of it just then, and it starts to rely on you, it's very powerful—feeling wanted by a baby tiger." The adult tigers stirred strong feelings in him as well, though more of respect and awe.

Pearce sees his character evolving through a series of conflicts to become a kind of intermediary between the human and tiger worlds in the film. "I think he's getting to the point in his life where he doesn't want to be doing this [hunting] any more. I imagined that he was cultivating more compassion for the animals that he was having to face off every day.

"Through Aidan, the audience gets to fall in love with the tigers as well," Pearce believes. "He's a sort of looking glass through which we get to see the effect on animals of what people do. His character provides an empathetic point of view, a link between what the animals are feeling and us as observers, understanding what they're feeling.

"And Jean-Jacques has captured the animals so sensitively and so beautifully that there is no way you can't be affected by their plight. It's just something about the way he shoots. You feel like you're really in the den with the tigers, living their life, experiencing what they experience."

There's a kind of balancing act in Annaud's films, says Pearce. "Jean-Jacques has a grand perspective on things that he contrasts so well with the small moments—you've only got to look at *Seven Years in Tibet* and other films he's done, which take in the sweeping enormity of the world, as well as its intimate nature. *Two Brothers* is very colorful and grand, the sets are extraordinary, and the enormous vistas looking across the jungle with the temples popping out. And then he'll move into the most intimate kind of moment between the two tiger cubs. It's so effective."

"The first time we met I knew Guy was the right person to play Aidan. The way he talked about the script, the way he talked about animals."

—JEAN-JACQUES ANNAUD

OPPOSITE: Annaud and Pearce confer while shooting the end of the temple raid.

Eugène Normandin JEAN-CLAUDE DREYFUS

The veteran French character actor Jean-Claude Dreyfus was born in Paris and at age eight gave his first performance in *La Jolie Meuniere de Maitre Jacques*. In his teens, he worked as a magician, but then decided to go into theater. He studied with the acclaimed acting teacher Tania Balachova until her death in 1973.

Since then he has performed for the theater, cinema, and television, also directing many of his own projects. Dreyfus is renowned for his ability to interpret difficult characters and for making apparently simple characters more complex. In 1992 he received a Cesar nomination for best supporting actor for his performance in Jean-Pierre Jeunet and Marc Caro's *Delicatessen*. His feature credits include *Lovely Rita, Rien Voila l'Ordre, L'Anglaise et le Duc (The Lady and the Duke), Tiré à part, The City of Lost Children, Cache-Cash, Le Fils de Gascogne,* and *Bonsoir*. In his *New York Times* review of Eric Rohmer's period romance *The Lady and the Duke*, A. O. Scott called Dreyfus's performance "passionate and restrained."

On television, he was most recently seen in *Maigret à l'école*. His prodigious theater career includes nominations for two best actor Moliere Awards, first in 1991 for *La Nonna* and again in 1998 for *Hygiene de l'assassin*.

"Normandin is one of the characters I adore," says Annaud. "He is the typical colonial administrator, sort of local governor of a French colony in Indochina—the colonial world I came to know from my military service and from researching *Black and White in Color*. They lose contact with their own world and create another world.

"Jean-Claude is a very experienced actor with a particular look that was perfect for my idea of this corrupt but genial colonial politician of a certain era. He reminds me of some of the famous lithographs by Honoré Daumier, caricatures of nineteenth-century political figures."

Madame Matilde Normandin
PHILIPPINE LEROY-BEAULIEU

Although Leroy-Beaulieu was born in France, she spent the first 11 years of her life in Italy with her father, the actor Philippe Leroy. Returning to France to complete high school, she went on to study literature at the Sorbonne. She became interested in theater and enrolled at the Conservatoire. Before the end of her first year, she was chosen to play Tawny for the television serial *L'amour en Héritage*, an ABC and France 2 co-production.

Like her opposite number, Jean-Claude Dreyfus, she has the kind of wide-ranging film and theater background that Annaud was seeking for his ensemble cast. Her film credits include Coline Serreau's *Trois Hommes et un Couffin* and its sequel *18 ans apres, TGV, Le Voie Est Libre, Hércule et Sherlock, La Belle Vert, Un Eroe Borghese, L'Année Juliette, Le Nez au Vent*, Andrzej Wajda's *Les Possédés*, Mehdi Charef's *Camomille*, Philippe Leguay's *Les Deux Fragonard*, Philippe de Broca's *Les Clés du Paradis*, Patrick Braoudé's *Neuf Mois*, and *A Soul Split in Two*. She also

appeared in James Ivory's *Jefferson in Paris* and Roland Joffé's *Vatel*. After making her theater debut in Molière's *l'Avare* with Michel Serrault, she appeared in Musset's *Les Caprices de Marianne*, in Musset's *Fantasio,* and recently in Pirandello's *On ne Sait Comment*.

Her French television credits also include *Sandra et le Siens*, a TV series, *Jean et la Loup, Mes Enfants Etrangers, Feu Sous la Glace, La Verité Est un Vilain Defaut*, and *Le Prix d'une femme*.

Raoul Normandin FREDDIE HIGHMORE

The young British actor Freddie Highmore will be seen in the upcoming feature *J. M. Barrie's Neverland*, which stars Johnny Depp, Kate Winslet, Dustin Hoffman, and Julie Christie. Highmore appeared in the miniseries *I Saw You, Jack and the Beanstalk: The Real Story, Mists of Avalon*, and *Happy Birthday Shakespeare*. He made his feature debut in *Women Talking Dirty*. Also due for release in late 2004 is a major film adaptation of Edith Nesbit's classic children's novel *Five Children and It*, in which Highmore stars alongside Kenneth Branagh, Zoe Wanamaker, and Eddie Izzard.

Aside from Guy Pearce, Highmore had more close contact with the tigers than any of the *Two Brothers* cast. The cubs who portrayed Sangha, his beloved pet, were bottle-raised and acclimated to a variety of humans, so being handled by a young boy was not a concern. The scene late in the film, however, where Raoul comes face to face with a fully grown Sangha, was created with a combination of blue screen work with real tigers and an animatronic stand-in. Highmore's performance, though, had to be as real as if a huge, live tiger stood inches away.

His Excellency OANH NGUYEN

Born in Saigon, Nguyen and his family were evacuated to the United States two days before the fall of South Vietnam. Oanh was raised in California, studied theater, and in 1997 founded the Chance Theater, where he serves as executive director.

Oanh made his feature debut in the film *Clockstoppers*. His theater credits include *De Donde, Blood Wedding, Love Letters, Skin of Our Teeth, The Hot L Baltimore*, and *Joseph and the Amazing Technicolor Dreamcoat*, where he met his wife, actress Erika Ceporious. For television his credits include roles in *Saved by the Bell, Hang Time, Kenan and Kel, Party of Five, The Beast*, and *Andy Richter Controls the Universe*.

He is also a playwright, usually directing his own works, which include *Undeclared, Is Pepperoni a Vegetable? and Other Mysteries of Love*, and *But I Don't Feel Grown-up*.

Paulette STÉPHANIE LAGARDE

The comic role of His Excellency's consort, Paulette, is deftly handled by Stéphanie Lagarde. Born in Limoges, Lagarde moved to Paris in 1984. She began attending dance classes but rebelled against schoolwork and decided to move to La Rochelle, where she studied under Colette Milner and discovered she had a talent for character roles. In 1986, she returned to Paris to attend drama school. In 1991 she traveled to Osaka, Japan, where she performed in a cabaret for seven months, returning to Paris to concentrate on her acting career.

Lagard's feature credits include *Sexes Très Opposés, Blind Date, Un Jeudi en Hiver, Vivre la Marée et la Liberation du Kurdistan*, and Jean-Luc Godard's *Forever Mozart*. Her television credits include *Taxi Blanc, Jalousie, Une Femme Piegée*, and *A Midsummer Night's Fire*. Among her theater credits are *Panique au Plaza* and *Le Beret de la Tortue*.

The Great Zerbino VINCENT SCARITO

Vincent Scarito was born in Belgium to Italian parents, and studied drama in Mons, Belgium. His feature film credits include *Le Roi Danse, Lumumba, Retour au Congo, Une Chance sur Deux*, and *Les Jolies Choses*. His television credits include the 1998 miniseries *The Count of Monte Cristo*.

Nai-Rea MAI ANH LE

Mai Anh Le was born in Paris to Vietnamese parents. She studied economics and management, while supporting herself by working as a model. She began her acting career in 2001 with the role of Akemi in Giodano Gederlini's feature film *Samourais*. The same year, she performed with Sandrine Bonnaire in *La Maison des Enfant*.

83

When Tigers Star

However well-crafted its script, however stunning its locations, however talented the actors playing human roles, the success of *Two Brothers* would hinge on its least predictable element: the performances of its feline stars. Wildlife documentaries have their place, but Jean-Jacques Annaud aimed for something else: a fictional drama in which tigers express love, hate, and fear; demonstrate loyalty and courage; overcome perils—in short, behave in ways that would enthrall audiences because people could recognize and share in those emotions and experiences. So casting and directing the tigers that would portray Sangha and Kumal at various stages in the story, and their parents, was the filmmakers' most critical task.

Fortunately Annaud knew, from his experience on *The Bear*, exactly who could find his leading actors and persuade them to perform as needed in front of the cameras. Head trainer Thierry Le Portier had worked with the director 15 years earlier on *The Bear* and more recently had worked on the Academy Award-winning *Gladiator*, along with U.S.-based trainer Randy Miller. Before even committing to make *Two Brothers*, Annaud consulted with Le Portier about the feasibility of his story.

"Jean-Jacques contacted me when he began writing the script," recalls Le Portier. "We talked a lot about many aspects of working with tigers. He was very interested in the different methods of training and how to get tigers to 'act.'

"Based on the script, I knew this would be the kind of movie that comes once in a lifetime for a trainer, because from beginning to end, the focus is on the tigers. I also knew it would be very difficult—having worked with Jean-Jacques, I know he insists on getting just the right images, without too much technical intervention. Most of the action people will see in *Two Brothers* is the tigers actually performing, alone or with other tigers—rather than composited together. We always went for the difficult way, not the easy way.

"But when I first read the script, I just read it like a story. I didn't want to begin by having to think: how will we do this or that? The hard part would come soon enough. My impression was that this story would be much more interesting and alive with action even than *The Bear*."

LEFT: *Tiger trainer Thierry Le Portier and a tiger cub.*

The Right Tiger for the Role

Careful casting is one of the most important aspects of Thierry Le Portier's job as head trainer for a film. Le Portier says, "If I make a mistake and choose the wrong animal, we might lose two or three hours of shooting time. If I choose the good one and it's a relatively simple shot, we're going to get what we need in 20 minutes. Obviously this is important to the director.

"I know the character of each of my tigers, and I know how they will react in different situations and to other tigers. For example, I have a big female tiger that is generally not afraid of anything. She is the one I would choose for difficult stunts. She is also very good with other tigers and particularly with the cubs."

Tigers vary widely in temperament and ability, which keeps the task interesting. "Some jump better than others; some prefer staying on the ground," says Le Portier.

"Some roar easily because they're more nervous. You can use that when you need a roar; for example, you give him an order but then stop him from doing it—like saying 'Come' but preventing him from coming forward. Because he's frustrated, he threatens you and you get the growl, but he's not going to attack. But a tiger with a stronger character won't roar so easily. If he does, he's probably ready to attack, so you cannot use him for growling on camera. You don't get the shot—and you have a problem!"

The film story called for tigers to interact in many ways: with affection, in play, and in battle. Getting unrelated tigers to relate as a family unit was tremendously challenging, especially in portraying the unique relationship between the mother and her cubs. For the scenes involving the tigress and cubs, Le Portier used one of his favorite tigers, Indra. "It was amazing—the baby tiger, which was not hers, played with her for 37 minutes, and she barely moved," he describes. "He played with her tail, batted at her, and eventually she even licked him. I was about five meters from her during the entire shot, and when she started to get annoyed with the cub, I calmed her down. To get that scene was a mix of the relationship I have with Indra, the orders I gave her, and the cub's natural instincts toward an adult female, even though she was not his mother."

Le Portier followed the script revisions, and before filming began, sat down for three days to talk through the tiger action with Annaud. "He had done storyboards and we talked for nine hours each day. Every shot was discussed with the director of photography and other crew members. Certain things Jean-Jacques wanted we knew would be very hard: for example, the longer the shot takes, and the wider the frame is, the most difficult it will be. The trainer must be far enough from the animal so he is not in the frame, and the animal must do his action for a long time—and even a few seconds is a long time for a tiger. On the other hand, some things that seemed very difficult on paper turned out to be not so bad."

Collaborating with Le Portier were his assistant trainer, Monique Angeon, and his former colleague Randy Miller, who brought two specially trained tigers from his operation in America. Miller, too, instantly recognized the project as a huge opportunity and a huge challenge. "A lot of the work that was expected from us and our animals had never been done—the scenes with tigers running or climbing on tricky terrain, chasing vehicles, running through the temples. But I felt very lucky to be involved. I don't think there's ever been a movie like this one—*The Bear* was terrific, but the animal performances in this are more complex."

Because Kumal and Sangha would be depicted at different ages, from young cub to full-grown adult, Le Portier had to assemble a large cast. "We used 30 tigers in all," says Le Portier. "Our biggest problem was to always have tiger cubs from seven to 12 weeks old, at the ready. We followed all the births, all over the world. Zoos were notified of our search and kept us up to date. We found most of our cubs in France and a few more in Thailand. Some were reared on a baby bottle. We picked up a lot of newborns that had been shunned by their mothers, a rather frequent phenomenon among tigresses."

Tiger Logistics

Preparation for taking the tigers to Cambodia had to begin months in advance of shooting. In addition to finding cubs and pregnant tigresses, the best method of transporting the tigers had to be worked. In addition, a great deal of research was done about how the tigers would react to the climate in Cambodia and what vaccinations and other medical protection would be required to keep them healthy. Despite the impression that tigers like hot weather, they prefer temperatures between 15° and 25° C (60° to 75°F).

The production arranged for the tigers to be transported from France to Cambodia about a month in advance so they could acclimatize before going to work. To provide the shortest, safest, and most comfortable travel conditions for them, Le Portier arranged for a cargo plane with a special pressurized, temperature-controlled cabin, and personally monitored the loading of the animals. Then he, along with Monique Angeon and unit manager Olivier Helie, accompanied the tigers on the journey, departing from a small airport in Vatry, France, on a direct flight to Siem Reap with only one short stopover for refueling. In Siem Reap, the production built a compound to house the tigers, constructed to the highest standards and kept scrupulously clean.

The terrain of each set, often covering several acres, had to be completely enclosed with special tiger-proof security nets, which were created by a local expert. Yves Herson was the unit manager in charge of controlling the animal shooting areas. Before filming began each day, he and his team patrolled the netting to ensure that there were no breaks. The tigers were allowed to roam freely within the perimeter of the nets, working with the trainers, while the filmmakers remained in cages. In some cases the nets were wound up and hidden at ground level so as not to appear in a shot—but if need demanded, they could be released in an instant, springing up dramatically to create a barrier.

Annaud recalls, "We spent our days in cages, behind bars and nets with the animals working around us. We set several cameras for each shot because we could never be exactly sure which way the tiger would go."

> "I knew this would be the kind of movie that comes once in a lifetime for a trainer, because from beginning to end, the focus is on the tigers."
>
> —*HEAD TRAINER THIERRY LE PORTIER*

ABOVE: *Guy Pearce and cubs with the team of trainers: Left to right, Hubert Wells, Anne Demazure, Pearce, Monique Angeon, Aline Ribet. Front row: Thierry Le Portier, Patrick Pittavino (dog trainer). Back row: David Faivre, Randy Miller.* OPPOSITE: *Annaud directs a shot of a cub climbing a tree. Far left is line producer Xavier Castano; far right, Thierry Le Portier.*

Even with all the precautions, tigers sometimes managed to go AWOL from a shot. "Sometimes there is nothing you can do because it happens too quickly," says Le Portier. "You may see it half a second before the tiger takes off, but you have no way to stop it. They didn't really escape because everywhere we shot was surrounded with a high net. But sometimes the area was large—two, three, or four acres of jungle or river or rocks—and then you go hunting tiger. They were always found quickly and brought back to the set. But on the next shot, he might try it again, because he enjoyed hiding in the trees, resting near the river. It's fun for the tiger, but not for the team who is stuck in cages waiting for us to find the tiger."

Getting Tigers to Act

Eliciting film performances from tigers requires a deep understanding of the animal's nature—as a species and as individuals—and exquisite coordination among trainers, director, and crew. Depending on what kind of acting is needed for a scene—expressive reactions, interaction with other animals, or vigorous action—the trainer may call on specific trained behav-

ABOVE: Le Portier works with a tiger in the open. Right: Annaud watches a scene from inside a mobile protective cage. OPPOSITE: The trainers took special care when eliciting emotional reactions from the tigers. OVERLEAF: Annaud and the camera crew set up a moving crane shot of the tigress trying to free Kumal; INSET: Trainer Randy Miller urges his tiger Shirkon to jump on the truck.

iors his animals have learned over several years (such as coming forward, stopping, or leaping), or an instinctive response to a stimulus or a surprise: what Randy Miller calls a "manipulated look."

Thierry Le Portier uses a combination of voice, sounds, and hand signals to direct the tigers. His methods rely on his ability to anticipate the tiger's moves, choose the correct tiger for the shot and being able to manipulate the tiger's natural behavior to fit the action. "You create a language common to you and the animal," he notes.

An endless supply of patience is essential as success is often a matter of being opportunistic, capturing the moment.

A scene like the tiger fight in the arena, which could not be convincingly created through compositing, had to unfold at its own pace. Two of Le Portier's male tigers, both dominant but not true enemies, were put in the arena together under close supervision. "They started by just coming together to sniff each other, and for a long time nothing happened; they just went off and lay down in the shade. Everyone was disappointed, but I told them, just be patient. Because after they are together in this small space for a while, one has to be

the boss. One began to test and provoke the other. Then we had something like a dance, because neither one was sure it was stronger. They started fighting or sparring, but it's like the first round of a boxing match, where each tests the other without going too far. When it would start to get too serious, I went in and separated them."

Drawing emotional reactions from grown tigers requires long experience in communicating with the animals and gauging their state of mind. Says trainer Randy Miller, "You can manipulate their expressions with your voice, body language, or using a prop that interests them. Tigers have a wide range of facial expressions, so it is possible to evoke looks that cover the full range of emotions."

Working with cubs versus adult tigers required very different techniques and expectations. As Le Portier points out, trying to train cubs would be like trying to train your three-month-old puppy: "It's playing all the time." So for the cubs, the primary technique was the manipulated look, or what Jean-Jacques Annaud called "method acting."

"Method acting is simply creating an emotion in an actor that is similar to the emotion that the character is feeling in the story," says the director. "I had a whole collection of things in my pocket that I used to attract the cubs' attention. For instance, if they sniff chocolate powder they sneeze immediately. Yawning was more difficult. We have several scenes where the little one gets tired and falls asleep. We had to plan for that. We knew that half an hour after they have had their bottle of milk, they really want to sleep, so you give them two bottles. Which makes them happy and they fall asleep, so you get the shot."

Le Portier's cubs were friendly with all the cast and crew members because they had been hand-raised

"A lot of the work that was expected from us and our animals had never been done—the scenes with tigers running or climbing on tricky terrain, chasing vehicles, running through the temples. But I felt very lucky to be involved. I don't think there's ever been a movie like this one."

—TRAINER RANDY MILLER

from birth by the trainer and his family, and bottle-fed from an early age. "All these babies were brought up with a bottle by my assistant, Monique, my daughter, my wife, or myself, starting months before the movie," he says. "But you don't want the cub to like you exclusively; it must be friendly with many people. So we take turns feeding them, and when visitors come, we let them play with the cubs and feed them. So for these babies, the whole human race are nice people."

Such close early knowledge of each individual also helps Le Portier with his casting choices. "When you know these animals well, you can see that this one is a little more courageous or curious; he wants to go places and do things. This other one holds back, is a little more afraid, but is very sweet with you and likes to be petted. And you use that for the movie."

Training a tiger for film work takes several years. "You start when he's about one year old," says Le Portier, "and by about age three he will be ready for a movie. At first you just do easy things, like getting him accustomed to being transported, to having cameras around and shooting, trolleys or cranes nearby. But the more complicated training for a difficult movie takes at least two years. I trained all my big tigers specifically for *Two Brothers*, but they were already trained to do many things."

The trainers used a variety of techniques to motivate grownup tigers for the intense action scenes, often using a moving lure like a feather or a piece of meat. Tigers tend to lose interest quickly, though (compared to a dog, say). In one scene, two tigers run together, each chasing a lure, but one or the other was likely to quit if it saw that its companion was winning the chase. In another action sequence, maybe the film's most dramatic, the mother tiger chases a truck carrying Kumal in a wooden crate lashed to the flatbed. Several tigers were used in that shot.

"With the bigger tigers, it's not so easy," Annaud observes. "You can attract their attention by having someone run away—say, on horseback—but you had better get it on the first take; because once the tiger has seen the horse outrun him, he isn't interested anymore.

"Day after day, Thierry came up with ideas to motivate the tigers to act in a way that works for the scene. He knows his animals, their instincts, their character and how they are going to react to each situation."

"I have an enormous respect for these animals," says Le Portier. "The relationship between a trainer and his animal is incredibly strong. You depend on him and he depends on you. He spends his whole life with you and is not only a friend, he is a colleague. Every shot is something that we do together. When we achieve a difficult shot, I can pet him a little and speak nicely to him and he understands that he did it right."

Le Portier is very aware that no matter how well trained his tigers are, they are still wild animals. "As soon as you step away, he is back to being a normal tiger with all of the tiger's ferocity. You cannot change their personalities, you can only add training. And captive tigers are dangerous—in some ways even more dangerous than wild tigers, because they are around people every day and are not frightened of them."

Guy Pearce recalls, "Obviously there came a point where we really couldn't work closely with the tigers, purely because of safety. I kept hearing Thierry's voice in my head saying, 'You can train them but you can't tame them.' So ultimately, I had a great deal of respect for that."

Le Poiter's affection for his dangerous charges is the enduring impression of their relationship. "If I didn't love tigers, I couldn't do this hard work for the six months we have been here. I've worked with big cats for more than 30 years, since I was 16."

"Method acting is simply creating an emotion in an actor that is similar to the emotion that the character is feeling in the story."

—JEAN-JACQUES ANNAUD

BELOW: Annaud and Le Portier set up a shot with the cub Kumal on the veranda of the village chief's house.

Movie Magic with a Light Hand

Because of the unpredictable nature of filming with animals, Annaud used a combination of high-definition digital (HD) and 35mm cameras. "Right from the preparation stage of *Two Brothers*, I thought it would be great to escape the drawbacks of 35mm that I had suffered on *The Bear*," he explains. "With animals it's vital to let the camera roll for long periods to capture the magic moments. They do the scenes well only once—if the cameras aren't rolling, you lose the light and the emotion forever.

"A year before we started production, I did a test comparing the best HD camera on the market with a 35mm camera. We spent two days shooting in different situations: landscapes, backlight, low light. I started out convinced that I had to do the whole movie on 35mm. But when I screened the footage of both formats with my team, none of us could tell the difference.

"Shooting on HD with the tigers made a huge difference. When I shot *The Bear* on 35mm, we had to change the film magazine every 12 minutes. The moment the bears started to do something interesting was always the moment when we had to stop to reload. It was so frustrating. With HD we can run for 50 minutes without stopping, and you can reload in less than five seconds, soundlessly, sometimes during a shot.

"For example, we had to stage a fight in the arena between the two brother tigers. We rolled for 25 minutes before anything happened, when suddenly they approached each other and started to fight. We got some fantastic images, then Thierry stepped in and stopped the fight before they could hurt each other. The odds are we would have missed it if we were shooting on 35mm."

Another point in favor of digital, says Annaud, is the ability to view rushes immediately—to verify what you've shot while you're still there and can start again if need be. "In this context, far from civilization, without any movie theaters around, 35mm would have forced me to do what I did with *The Lover*: see the rushes three weeks later. Too late to do anything about it!"

Finally, digital required less light. "To shoot in the temples at night, we lit several acres with six helium-filled balloons lit from the inside. This method is infinitely more subtle. It allows you to spread natural-looking light over vast expanses, eliminating the nightmare of hundreds of projectors to be calibrated and masked.

"Nevertheless," Annaud continues, "we did shoot a few scenes in 35mm. Our prototype digital cameras did not have slo-mo. To capture the look in the tigers' eyes, it's often necessary to work at 120 images per second."

While the overwhelming majority of the shots were live action, the filmmakers used animatronic tigers for any shots in which the tigers' safety and comfort would be compromised. "We used animatronic shots where shooting live action with a real

OPPOSITE: The tigers used for the arena scene begin to fight but were quickly separated.

"The relationship between a trainer and his animal is incredibly strong. You depend on him and he depends on you. He spends his whole life with you and is not only a friend, he is a colleague. Every shot is something that we do together."

—*THIERRY LE PORTIER*

Animatronics

In the climactic scene where Kumal and Sangha are set against each other in the arena, Sangha turns on the circus tamers with terrifying results. For obvious safety reasons, this scene made use of animatronics: meticulously crafted mechanical tigers controlled by animators. Heading the animatronics team was Pascal Molina, who notes, "To realize that effect we used a combination of shots. Shots of a real tiger attacking a dummy were intercut with shots of a mechanical tiger jumping on the actor."

The key to making any animatronic effect look believable is time, says Molina. "You need time to make the original sculptures, to make the eyes and teeth, and refine the mechanics. But what really takes time is hair. We work with natural hair, implanting it clump by clump, almost hair by hair." Molina's team created five full-size tigers, three heads, and several partial cubs. They also made paws and tails for closeups, to give the real tigers a rest, as well as three human dummies, 60 ducks, piglets, civets, goats, turtles, and chickens. It took four people to operate the animatronic tiger heads.

Animatronics were also used in the scenes where the tigress carries the cubs in her mouth. "Since the tigress was not the cub's real mother, we had to use a fake head carrying a real cub and a real tiger carrying a fake cub," says Molina. To train Indra to carry the fake cub, Thierry Le Portier gave it to her as a toy. She became quite attached to it, taking the "cub" back into her den after the scene was done and refusing to part with it. It took several attempts by trainers Le Portier and Monique Angeon to extract it from her jaws, and not without damage.

Molina was most impressed by the trainers' work. "When the audience sees the film, they will think that a lot of the scenes used animatronics, which is nice for me. However, the reality is that 99 percent of the shots used real animals. We were just there to avoid unnecessary stress on the tigers."

tiger would be impossible," says Annaud. "For instance, we used a combination of animatronic and VSFX shots for the scene where the tigers are trapped by fire in the jungle. The fire was never close to the tigers. The flames were placed near the cameras for one portion of the shots, and these were enhanced by visual effects in post-production. The tigers jumped from one rock to another, and never through the flames."

Compositing was used for most of the shots in which human characters and tigers appear in the same frame, as well as some where it was impossible to shoot two or more tigers together in the same frame. A motion-control camera was used to exactly replicate the camera moves so that the shots could be assembled.

Other than the composite shots, the use of visual effects was minimal. Notes VSFX supervisor Frédéric Moreau, "Our work on this film was guided by the constraints of realism. It was important that none of the scenes which passed through our hands could be differentiated from the scenes that are purely shot through the camera."

Most of the VSFX work involved adding subtle touches. For example, a flight of bats from the temple had to be created digitally because the local species is protected.

"For shots using animatronics, we intervened pretty rarely," notes Moreau. "They are controlled by the animators themselves, though we sometimes add a little movement."

Moreau didn't mind at all that his work stays in the background in this film. "Jean-Jacques makes our work joyous. We go a lot further than he asks because our working relationship is based on such humor and mutual confidence. And we have beautiful images to work with."

During the location scouting, Annaud had photographed hundreds of sites using a large-format camera: Cambodian architecture, landscapes, colonial buildings, and so on. Using digital technology, these images enriched certain moments in the film—a mountain added behind a plain, a village in perspective, palm trees in a landscape. This style took its inspiration from the Düsseldorf School painters, who made sketches from nature and then mingled elements from various landscapes on a single canvas.

Without animatronics or VSFX, about 40 shots vital to the picture could never have been made. Taken together, however, they amount to only a minute of edited film. The miracle of computer-aided effects is celebrated in many movies these days, but *Two Brothers* celebrates a different kind of achievement. "On this movie," says Thierry Le Portier fervently, "it's a miracle every day."

OPPOSITE, BOTTOM: The "real" and the dummy Zerbino in the attack scene with animatronic tiger. OPPOSITE, TOP: An animatronic tiger head was used to carry a real cub here; in other shots, a real tigress carries a fake cub. RIGHT: A combination of visual effects and animatronics was used for the scene near the end of the film when Raoul takes the collar off the adult Sangha.

The Journey Is the Reward

Creating a film like *Two Brothers* is a journey with a very long arc—nearly five years in this case. Jean-Jacques Annaud began his research in 1998, and he first sat down with Alain Godard to work on the screenplay in 1999. After pausing to finish work on *Enemy at the Gates*, Annaud made location scouting trips in 2001. Casting and other pre-production work occupied most of 2002, and the project reached its sustained climax in an eight-month shoot beginning in October 2002. Once principal photography wrapped at Paris's Arpejon Studios in June 2003, cast and crew scattered, leaving Annaud to orchestrate a graceful denouement with the all-important editing, sound editing, and scoring of the film.

Certain aspects of the production stood out memorably for all involved. Above all, shooting in Cambodia gave the film its identity; this saga shaped many lives for a year or more. Surrendering to the romance of the Angkor temples was easy. Building an infrastructure that would allow a film crew of 400-plus to function in half-a-dozen locations around Cambodia—a country that does not even have an official film commission and is still recovering from massive civil strife—was another matter entirely.

Line producer Xavier Castano was the chief organizer, strategizer, diplomat, and cheerleader for the Cambodian journey. "At the beginning I didn't know if we could do this movie because I knew at once what an enormous undertaking it would be. If I hadn't made *The Bear* with Jean-Jacques, I would never had started. Even though our past experience made it more comfortable, this movie is harder because it is in Asia."

Annaud had already laid the groundwork. "We were fortunate to have funding for an extended pre-production period because we needed that time to explain to the Cambodians what we were going to do. Six months before the shoot I went there to meet with the authorities about our project. We met the king and the prime minister; it was very friendly. I said, we don't need anything except your cooperation, and on our side we're going to try to help you to understand what we're doing and try to teach Cambodians to work on a film crew.

"It's a different approach. You cannot just arrive there, rent a crew, rent cars, get the hotels. You talk to the hotel owners a year in advance. You see the local authorities in charge of the temples and explain what you want to do. If we had come in with a different attitude, we would not have gotten permission to shoot where we did."

Just setting a start date for the shoot was a feat of timing to coordinate key factors: when the country would be politically calm enough, when tiger births were scheduled, when the temples could be closed

"I always have the feeling when I start my films: This one's going to be a small one. Just two tigers in the jungle. And then I end up with 300 trucks somewhere in the middle of Cambodia."

—JEAN-JACQUES ANNAUD

Behind the Cameras

The length of the Cambodia shoot and its daunting conditions were a factor in reshuffling Annaud's core group of production heads, a team that had been remarkably consistent through several movies. Production designer At Huong was lost due to illness, to be replaced by Pierre Queffelean. Another new face on the team was director of photography Jean-Marie Dreujou.

Annaud explains: "With my previous DP, Robert Fraisse, I did four films and I thought he would be part of this one. But he was concerned about my decision to shoot primarily with High Def, which he had not worked with. Also, I think he did not want to spend so much time in Cambodia. He knows me and has been on difficult locations with me before!

"I was delighted that Jean-Marie took the job, and I'm sure we will collaborate again.

He is quite famous in France, having done beautiful photography on several films for Pierre LeConte, such as *Monsieur Hire, The Girl on the Bridge*, and *Ridicule*. He has been a terrific 'acquisition' for me, doing remarkable work under very difficult conditions, and he never complained. He understands the needs of storytelling, and that is so rare. He doesn't think image first; he thinks story, and images for the story. And therefore light for the image for the story."

A key factor in the cinematography was how quickly the light changes in Cambodia, which can cause headaches for continuity. Dust and haze often came into play as the land dried out after the rainy season. The biggest decisions, of course, were where to put cameras to capture the best moments with the tigers. "The key is to be patient and to use multiple cameras. I always put my favorite camera where I feel the best angle should be. But then the animal may decide to take a different position," says Annaud.

"It's complicated by the fact that we were shooting wide screen, anamorphic, so there is a lot of field. We sometimes had to hide cameras in cages or use remote-controlled cameras. And this was not a little video camera; we're shooting with High Def and 35mm cameras—not many remote systems can handle such heavy equipment. Still, we usually managed to have three or four cameras. I know that I'm going to be successful on a scene if my cameras are widely deployed."

LEFT: *Director of photography Jean-Marie Dreujou peers out from his protective cage.*

to visitors, when the landscape would look its best. "The quality of the vegetation and the light is so fantastic, we needed to start a month before the end of the rainy season," Castano explains. "But there was a danger that the rainy season would last longer than normal."

Obtaining permission to shoot in and around the temples, in the national park at Phnom Koulen, and in the heart of Phnom Penh, had Castano working through myriad channels, official and unofficial. "I had to develop close personal relationships with members of the Cambodian government. The help and encouragement they gave us was outstanding."

A number of film technicians traveled to Asia with the production, but the filmmakers also had to rely on local resources. Assembling a crew in Cambodia, where few feature films have been shot, was a challenge, but they succeeded beyond their hopes. Castano recalls, "We advertised on the radio and in the newspapers, resulting in 500 applicants a day. In all, we employed more than 400 local people, allocating them among various departments. Obviously, translation was important so we hired a lot of Cambodians who could speak some French or English."

"It worked fantastically well," says Annaud. "The Cambodian unit was absolutely superb. They learned incredibly fast and are now as competent as any international unit I've worked with."

Castano adds, "I brought about 14 people from France to run the art department; each took on 10 local people and taught them to help build the sets and re-create the statues. A small local company makes sculptures for the tourist trade; a few years ago it started a school, and we employed some of those students. Many of the statues they made have been donated to the National Museum in Phnom Penh."

The production welcomed any help that would smooth their way, because the jungle conditions were enormously taxing for the cast, crew, and tigers. Temperatures ranged from 30° to 35°C (85° to 95°F) with 100 percent humidity. In the more remote locations, great care had to be taken to avoid poisonous snakes and insects. One crew member was stung by a scorpion; another had a close encounter with a tarantula. A six-foot python even visited the set one day. All the Europeans received a full range of vaccinations before coming to Asia, but nevertheless many succumbed to a mild case of typhoid not long after arriving. "We had been vaccinated, of course," says Annaud, "but the germ can vary, and we were not protected from this one."

Castano's chief concern was how the tigers would react to the extreme heat. "I was very worried that they would not be able to perform the action in the script, so I worked very hard to make their lodgings as comfortable as possible. Without the tigers, the movie doesn't exist."

ABOVE: *Annaud on the Ta Prohm set with local extras.*
RIGHT: *Line producer Xavier Castano behind the camera.*

Far and Away

Around the well-touristed temples of Angkor and the hotels of Siem Reap, it wasn't obvious that Cambodia was quite recently a war-torn land. But the when the production moved to the mountainous region of Phnom Koulen, it came home to them in a hurry. This rugged, densely forested area—home to a famous mountaintop shrine—was the final stronghold of the Khmer Rouge leaders, who held out there until 1998. In 1992 some 600 Cambodians a month were killed or maimed by land mines and unexploded ordinance. The Cambodian government and the UN established the Cambodian Mine Action Center (CMAC) to free the people from this threat, but despite their efforts, an estimated 4 to 6 million mines still remain hidden in Cambodia.

Explains Castano, "Because the area was still full of mines, we had to employ a complete CMAC de-mining unit a month before we were scheduled to shoot there. It was especially complicated because normally they clear all the vegetation before beginning to de-mine, but we needed virgin landscape for our film. Finally we worked out a way to de-mine the area thoroughly without cutting the vegetation. After we began shooting, we kept the CMAC unit with us as a precaution." The crew was constantly warned not to stray from the marked, de-mined areas.

In order even to access Phnom Koulen with their equipment, the production had to construct new roads, including 10 bridges, which took two months to complete. Despite the improved roads, Phnom Koulen was over an hour and half by car from Siem Reap.

One of the scenes in Phnom Koulen portrayed Aidan leading a tiger hunt for the Prince from the backs of elephants. The elephants came from Angkor, where they normally carry tourists to the top of Bak Kheng temple to watch the sunset. For three days, their keepers rode on the elephants from Siem Reap all the way to Phnom Koulen, camping out in the jungle at night.

The most dramatic scenes shot in Phnom Koulen were those in which Kumal and Sangha, near the end of the film, are trapped by a ring of fires. The production obtained permission to set small, carefully controlled fires in strategic locations, their effect maximized by VSFX and lots of smoke.

Phnom Koulen also contains the high overlook from where Kumal and Sangha gaze down at their domain at the end of the film. The great temple they see rising up through the jungle below does exist, though it has been cinematically transposed into this landscape.

If Phnom Koulen seemed remote, it was actually well-traveled compared to the production's last location in Cambodia. This was a village called Putong

LEFT: *The Mondol Kiri set from the chief's house, with a stand-in cub.* OPPOSITE: *Annaud, cast, and elephants in the tiger hunt scene in Phnom Koulen.*

in the mountain province of Mondol Kiri, on the country's eastern frontier near Vietnam. The Phnong tribes-people who live here are isolated from mainstream Cambodia, providing the production with both a setting and a group of extras that looked as if they could have stepped out of a past century.

Explains production designer Pierre Queffelean, "The Phnong do not speak Khmer, the dominant Cambodian language, and they have a totally different culture and way of life. We tried to re-create that in the sets."

The art department arrived in Putong several weeks ahead of the rest of the crew to work on the sets: mostly buildings created in the traditional local style. "We showed the Phnong drawings, and they constructed the buildings themselves," Queffelean continues. "We gave them everything they needed: equipment, wood, straw, which they braided for the roofs—and they built the houses beautifully. They brought their own style to the design, adding features we would never come up with. The traditional building materials are bamboo and straw, which we could find locally, but we also used resin and polystyrene imported from France and Thailand."

Built as permanent structures, the houses were donated to the villagers, with the village chief responsible for deciding their allocation.

While the sets were being readied, so were accommodations for the cast and crew. There are no hotels in Mondol Kiri, so the production constructed a village of 120 tents. Working with a hotel engineer, they arranged a system to provide hot and cold water, with a filtration system to purify water taken from a nearby lake. Waste water was disposed of by using a design invented in refugee camps, whereby the water is naturally filtered through rocks and sand and returned into the ground.

Creature comforts were minimal, however, and daytime temperatures in Mondol Kiri rose as high

"The Cambodian unit was absolutely superb. They learned incredibly fast and are now as competent as any international unit I've worked with."

—JEAN-JACQUES ANNAUD

as 45°C (115°F). The misery was amplified by clouds of fine red dust that got into the camera, the recording equipment, eyes, noses, throats—everything. Fortunately, there were several night shoots in Putong when the temperature was more bearable. These attracted a large crowd, though not necessarily to watch the filming. The set was lit up with large lighting balloons, and people came from miles around to take advantage of the light for a social evening, since ordinarily there is no electricity at night.

Life on Location

In a short documentary feature about making *Two Brothers*, the set for the market scene in central Phnom Penh is deluged with late monsoon rain. Wading across a flooded street to take cover in a canvas stall, Jean-Jacques Annaud comments with a grin on the joys of filmmaking on location: "Why stay in the studio when you can have this?"

How did the director himself cope with the pressure of making a major film with so many unknown factors, under such strenuous conditions? The short answer is: he thrives on it. As Xavier Castano notes wryly, Annaud was in his element in circumstances like these. "To shoot in Mondol Kiri, for instance, to build a camp like that, it is an adventure. I am sure it was the best part of the film for him."

Interviewed after the hundredth day of the Cambodian shoot, with another 50 days still to complete, Annaud says, "I have not been back to my country since September and we are now at the end of March. So I've been away shooting every day, but I'm very happy. Once in a while, I think, oh, yeah, am I crazy?

"I always have the feeling when I start my films: This one's going to be a small one. Just two tigers in the jungle. And then I end up with 300 trucks somewhere in the middle of Cambodia. Probably it's because when I think about the story, it's always just about a few characters. But I love movies, I like the big screen; I like to fill up the screen with images of my dreams. That's why it always starts small and grows."

The longer answer to how Annaud copes is that he knows how to prepare for such epics, who to bring along to make it all work, and how to keep his crew happy on the set. "A big part of my job is to create a good atmosphere, to nurture a positive sense of teamwork. A set is a matter of seduction."

It's also a matter of clearly communicating the director's desires and expectations to a large, diverse group of people, in a way that stirs and sustains their own enthusiasm. "I learned in my early days as a director of commercials for TV how important good communication on the set is. I realized that the key for a director was to make sure that everyone in my crew, every single person, knew what I had in my head, even very far back in my head. So finding ways to do this became very important for me.

The director with his illustrated script in Mondol Kiri.

Le Petit Journal

O ne of Annaud's favorite ways to keep in touch with his crew on location is to publish a newsletter every day—or as often as possible—about what is being shot, who is visiting the set, what special concerns might arise during filming that day. He called it *Le Petit Journal*, after the name of a popular colonial-era news gazette that often featured accounts of adventure in faraway lands. Another was the *Journal des Voyages*. European readers eagerly followed the perils of intrepid explorers and big-game hunters in these periodicals, and Annaud used them as inspiration for sets, costumes, and atmosphere.

"I would change the title of the publication depending on the location where we were," notes Annaud. "And very often I put in a picture related to the scene we're going to shoot. People were happy to have this because they could see the connection between what they read, what they were about to do, and what we're going to get on screen. It keeps everyone in the crew 'on the same page,' so to speak."

Pages from Annaud's Petit Journal *newsletter published on the set, and a cover from the old* Journal des Voyages, *one of his models.*

LE POISSON

La crèce du jour

N° 107   Le 1 Avril 2003

Où il est annoncé qu'un jour on finira par quitter les arènes. Poisson d'Avril.

Note: le découpage théorique des scènes est donné ici pour mémoire. On l'adaptera aux réalités changeantes du moment.

Mes amis Cambodgiens. C'était le bon temps.

Scène 84 (Le VIEUX TIGRE poussé vers la piste assiste à son triomphe en coulisses)

MOTION CONTROL double passe. Caméra près de la cage de Kumal. Pano accompagnant la descente PL du VIEUX TIGRE de sa cage, son déplacement nonchalant vers le tunnel, son arrêt devant le petit tigre PR et son regard vers lui.

- 2ème caméra: LOCK-OFF à l'intérieur de la cage de KUMAL qui bouffe en avant-plan tandis que le VIEUX TIGRE passe et s'arrête pour contempler le succès de son remède.

- 3ème caméra: LOCK-OFF à l'intérieur du tunnel.

- 4ème caméra: long de la roulotte face à la cage du V...

caméra proche de la cage du ...age continue son chemin en ... rabrouer, fait le détour pour ...arque un dernier regard vers

LE RÉSIDENT

Le bulletin des occupants du plateau 4   Jeudi 23 Mai 2003

N° 198

Où, grâce à la participation d'un aquarium kamikaze et la bonne volonté d'un poisson rouge cascadeur il est envisageable de renouer avec les plaisirs nautiques d'antan.

Scène 103 (Les notables et le poisson rouge dans la tornade)

PL dessus de la maquette: NORMANDIN et les notables assis en arc de cercle, avec amorce de poisson rouge qui évolue dans son bocal. LOCK-OFF. (Faire la passe à vide AVANT le passage des animaux et le désastre conséquent.)

PA en dessous de la maquette: LOCK-OFF avec passage du tigre et du chien. (Faire la passe à vide AVANT le passage des animaux et le désastre conséquent.)

PR simultané en pano sur le tigre

PR simultané en pano sur le chien

PR simultané sur le notable proche du bocal

Détail de la statue qui vacille et choit.

"I write and send a lot of notes; I like my unit to know what I have besides the screenplay. And precisely because I am the kind of director who prepares a lot up front, I absolutely adore coming to meetings with piles of photographs and explaining my ideas at length. Every day they receive papers with illustrations and notes to describe what I want. Because if I don't tell them today what I need in 50 days, I'm not going to get it in 50 days.

"Young filmmakers sometimes are very innocent. They think they can just get on the set and create spontaneously. But on what set will they arrive? On a set that resembles what they dreamed, or something less than that? Unless you have been careful about planning these details, your imagination cannot be free to create on the set. For me, at least.

"A different problem can arise when people you have worked with for a long time assume you want

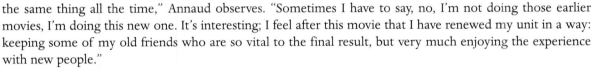

the same thing all the time," Annaud observes. "Sometimes I have to say, no, I'm not doing those earlier movies, I'm doing this new one. It's interesting; I feel after this movie that I have renewed my unit in a way: keeping some of my old friends who are so vital to the final result, but very much enjoying the experience with new people."

A very familiar face on all the director's projects is his wife, continuity supervisor Laurence Duval-Annaud. The two met on the set of *Coup de Tête* in 1987, and she has been a constant collaborator ever since. "I would not do a movie if she did not like the script because I trust her to be honest," he says. "After a certain amount of success people tend to flatter you, and you don't get a useful response. With her I don't have this problem at all.

"We have a quite magnificent relationship on the set—she's not only doing her job as continuity supervisor, she also has a very good eye for frames and acting and for the meaning of images. Often she is stationed in front of the monitor to see what we are getting—because I am with the actors. It is my rule always to be with my actors, whether two-legged or four-legged; I'm with them near the camera, feeling the same wind, the same smoke. I feel that's very important to my way of working.

"So at the end of a shot I might ask her, 'Did you see that moment where the tiger looked so angry?' and through the intercom she will reply, 'Yes, but it was out of focus, but there was another good moment . . .' and so on. Together we decide if we have achieved the shot, and Laurence makes a note for [editor] Noelle Boisson, saying precisely what we liked and why."

Typically Annaud would review his impressions of the day's work and make notes for future reference while he and Laurence drove back to their hotel, about an hour and a half from the set in most cases. I'm very grateful that we can work together so well. We never get angry at each other; it's quite miraculous. We have dinner together and we don't speak about the movie."

ABOVE: Laurence Duval-Annaud with Jean-Jacques Annaud, Guy Pearce, and Thierry Le Portier.

Putting It All Together

Two Brothers wrapped in mid-June 2003 at Arpejon Studios outside Paris, with Annaud and company finishing the shots of Aidan McRory attending a London antiquities auction—one of the very first scenes in the film but the last to be recorded.

Not long after that, Annaud began spending much of his time in a state-of-the-art editing facility, working with his long-time film editor Noelle Boisson. "Noelle and I went to the same film school and started as kids together in commercials," he says. "She has been my editor for 30 years, and we have great complicity together. She's now regarded as a star among editors in France and has worked on many great movies, but she has been very faithful to me over the years. This partnership is so important that she is always the first person outside the financier to whom I show the script."

Nominated for an Academy Award for her work on The Bear, Boisson also collaborated with Annaud on Seven Years in Tibet, The Lover, and Coup de Tête. Her other credits include Cyrano de Bergerac, starring Gerard Depardieu, Vatel, The Bridge, A Soldier's Daughter Never Cries, Jean de Florette, Shadow Play, The Horseman on the Roof, and The Machine.

Clearly it's a unique editing challenge to take Annaud's hard-won footage of animals performing and weave it into a coherent dramatic story. "I consider the editing process a rewrite," Annaud declares. "We have to look at the images not for what they are meant to be but for what they really convey, and then restructure as necessary based on the feeling we get from those images. Noelle is terrific at this, and it helps that we've known each other so long. She's a very tough judge and will always tell me—in a diplomatic, charming way—if something isn't good."

Boisson is never present on the set, however. "She doesn't want to know how the images are made," Annaud explains. "She wants to see the result, and to experience only her reactions to that footage. And then put it together to tell the story she knows I want to tell. She is not prejudiced by knowing about the difficulties that went into getting a shot, and I don't want her to know. If a terrible image required two days of work, it has to go in the dustbin. On the contrary, if a moment from an outtake that was not even supposed to be in the movie has some magic, it deserves to be considered."

"I think because I started so young as a director and have done so much work, I'm quite content to dismiss two days or two weeks of work at this point," he muses. "I am not attached to what I have shot—if it's not good, it should go. I want to show what means something. With age and experience you can edit yourself more freely—sometimes it even feels like a strange pleasure to cut off a limb in this way!"

Sound editing is the next key step after a rough cut of the visuals has been completed. In this film, it was an especially critical step to support the storytelling—as with any actor, the tigers' performance would be composed of visual expressions, movement, and vocalizing. To his great relief and pleasure, Annaud discovered in his research that tigers have an enormous range of vocal expression.

> "Realisateur is a better word than 'director.' Because you are not just giving direction, you are bringing something into being that did not exist. Realizing some possibility."
>
> —JEAN-JACQUES ANNAUD

"They have a much greater vocabulary of sounds than domestic cats. Even dogs don't make as many different sounds. As I learned, this is because tigers are usually solitary animals with large territories, and it's vital that they can communicate over long distances—making phone calls, if you like. They also have a whole range of softer sounds, for when they don't want to be overheard. For instance, if a mother is hunting and leaves her little ones behind, she makes sounds to reassure them, or remind them to stay still.

"We created a list and recordings of 50 different sounds to provide to our sound editors. So when we wanted to convey a particular emotion or mood, we could ask for a prusten [a kind of hoarse puffing sound] instead of a purr, or a distant 'aaoum' instead of a roar."

The final layer of atmosphere and drama was added, as usual, by the musical soundtrack. As tiger trainer Thierry Le Portier observes, this too was part of completing the tigers' performance. "Because, of course, tigers do not speak, and we rely on interpreting their expressions—on what we see in the frame and also what we hear. So the emotions communicated through the music will be very important."

But as Annaud well knew, using music to convey emotion requires a fine hand. "It's very tricky to score a film with animals—it can so easily be heavy-handed or sentimental. Before getting the final score, we had to do some screenings with temporary music, and even though I had a music editor with whom I had worked on other movies, we struggled for weeks and weeks. Nothing was fitting, and I was petrified."

"I chose Stephen Warbeck to do the music because I liked what he did for other movies so much, especially *Shakespeare in Love*," says Annaud. (Oscar voters agreed, deeming Warbeck's music for that film the best original score of 1998.) "His melodies were so inventive and the orchestration light and subtle. Although I have always been lucky with musicians, having worked with great movie composers like John Williams, James Horner, and Gabriel Yared, I must say that this has been my best experience so far. I'm absolutely delighted with this music and with the relationship we formed. He's a great melodist and does his own orchestration. Besides, he's a man of great tenderness, humor, and charm!"

In addition to *Shakespeare in Love,* Warbeck's feature credits include *Captain Corelli's Mandolin, Billy Elliot, Mrs. Brown, Mystery Men, Quills,* and *Birthday Girl.* He has also written music for more than 40 television series, including PBS's highly successful *Prime Suspect,* and holds the position of Head of Music and Associate Artist at the Royal Shakespeare Company. His notable stage productions include the National Theatre's *An Inspector Calls,* John Madden's production of *Proof,* Sam Mendes' production of *To the Green Fields Beyond, The Triumph of Love,* and the Royal Shakespeare Company's *The White Devil.*

A director who cares deeply about music, Annaud found everything going his way this time. "The process was so smooth and full of fun and friendship, and I'm enchanted with the results."

ABOVE: *The brother tigers from the film vocalize at a trainer's prompting.*

Sounds of Asia

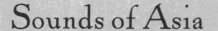

"I knew Stephen Warbeck was the right choice for this film when I visited him at his farm in England, where he lives with lots of animals," Annaud relates. "I found him surrounded by an amazing collection of Asian instruments that he has owned for years. I very much wanted to use these sounds in the score and was so glad Stephen was excited about this, too. As we talked, he would say, 'Wait, we should try this sitar!' and suddenly he would be on his knees playing one.

"But it's always difficult to make fusion music successfully, and I feel Stephen is extremely talented at it. This music will have a unique personality. We are using melodies that have a strong Asian perfume." Some of the unusual instruments featured are the sheng, a kind of harmonica that sounds like a cross between an accordion and panpipes. Also used were the pipa, which resembles a lute or mandolin; various Asian flutes such as the cheng; and percussion instruments including gongs, gamelan, and an Asian xylophone. "The way he has blended them is so nice."

Annaud adds, "We also recorded the so-called 'source music'—background music—with an ensemble of Cambodian musicians. They play a charming version of the old French tune *Plaisir d'Amour*. And we have a little choir of Indochinese children singing a version of *La Marseillaise* to welcome the Prince in one scene. We wrote special lyrics for this rendition, closely related to the original but with a local flavor, in Cambodian.

Last Words

Shortly before winding up his Cambodian sojourn, Annaud offered some thoughts about what made this production special—and why he works so hard to make every film that way.

"I think the reason we have been so happy working on this movie is that everyone felt there was some magic—about these animals and how we relate to them, and about the place where we are working. All my crew say they want to return to Cambodia. But it's also because we have had such a friendly feeling among us. There has to be a lot of discipline on this set—if one person is moving and the tiger is distracted, he'll never perform the action. But my unit has been wonderful. And they all are impressed to see that, day after day after day we are filming things in the script they doubted could be done."

Realizing the impossible is Annaud's specialty, of course. In fact, the term he much prefers to "director" is its French equivalent: *réalisateur*. "It's a better word. Because you are not just giving direction, you are bringing something into being that did not exist. Realizing some possibility."

"My problem is always to fulfill a passionate desire," he explains. "It's like falling in love, you know? For years you may see all kinds of women, but you're fine with your newspaper or your book—then suddenly, you want *that one*. Well, I'm that way: Suddenly, nothing is too expensive or too difficult. But I need to be possessed fully by this desire; if not, I don't think I would have the courage to face the ordeal of shooting for so many days.

"The passion and the fun are essential for me. To keep the analogy with lovemaking, without passion it is not fun. And you don't do it well. But when you have the intense desire to tell a story, and then get the reward of putting on screen what was in your head, it's a wonderful translation of your inner passions.

"I also have to convince my unit that it will be rewarding for them. If you work with a crew day after day, and they are not convinced that they're doing something special—they are only there to make money—it's not satisfying for anyone. The best thing is when I have the feeling that my crew is flying with me. That's a wonderful feeling; that's my life."

OPPOSITE: Pages from the Two Brothers *score composed by Stephen Warbeck show his unique instrumentation. Photos show musicians at the scoring sessions for the film and (inset) Warbeck with his score as he confers with conductor Nick Ingman. RIGHT: The children's chorus led by Nai-Rea (Mai Anh Le) performs a modified version of* La Marseillaise.

Once Upon a Time in the Jungle

The Story in Images

Based on the Film by
Jean-Jacques Annaud
with Alain Godard

~ 1 ~
In Which Our Tigers Are Born
and the Great Hunter Finds a New Quarry

A century ago, deep in the jungles of Southeast Asia, tigers live at peace among the forgotten ruins of fantastic temples. Stone Buddhas, their feet trapped in the tentacles of the encroaching forest, smile down on a beautiful tigress and her young cubs, safe in their den in the heart of the temple. Kumal and Sangha are beginning to venture out and discover their world, full of intriguing fellow creatures, trees to climb, and enchanting playthings like a tumbling coconut or their mother's twitching tail. Nearby patrols their father, the Great Tiger, who rules this domain; now and then he joins his family to rest and cool off by the river, whose waters splash over sacred images graven into the rocky bed.

But their sanctuary does not remain peacefully forgotten. Thousands of miles away, a passion for ancient treasures has swept the western world. At an auction in far-off London, a romantic adventurer named Aidan McRory, famous for writing books about his big-game-hunting exploits, watches in disbelief as his hard-won African ivory is ignored while a small Buddha head brings thousands under the gavel. McRory, grown weary of the slaughter in any case,

lusts after a share of the loot and travels to Indochina, where he assembles a local crew and leads an expedition to pillage the temples.

Tigress and cubs awake from slumber one morning to the *boom* of explosives bringing the giant Buddha crashing to earth. Ever protective, the mother quickly retreats, carrying Sangha to safety—but before she can return for Kumal, McRory's dog has raised the alarm. The Great Tiger, who has been standing sentry, leaps out from hiding and attacks Aidan's servant, in the lead. Right behind him, though, is the great hunter, who shoulders his rifle and kills the huge beast. As they pull his body away, Kumal is revealed, shaking with fear but standing his ground, growling defiantly in his baby tiger voice.

Amused, Aidan lowers his weapon. Rather than kill the cub, he decides to take Kumal back to the village he's made his base of operations, as an offering—along with the dead tiger's hide—for the village chief. As the expedition wends its slow way out of the jungle, laden with priceless stone artifacts and a 500-pound tiger, Aidan rides atop a cart with the cub in his lap. The young animal has already bonded to him . . . and the hunter feels his heart beginning to melt like the honey drops in water he has fed to Kumal.

When Kumal and Sangha are a few weeks old, their mother takes them to the river near the temple, where the river rocks are carved with sacred images. The Great Tiger waits there, and meets his cubs for the first and only time. The parents watch as their offspring play in the water.

A *fallen coconut becomes a prized plaything for the brothers, who chase it down a slope and wrestle to see who gets to keep the prize.*

A bone-chilling roar shakes the ruins. The Great Tiger leaps out from behind the rock pile. In a second he is all over Napolean, planting his claws in the flesh of his shoulders, pinning him to the ground.

Kumal sees another upright shadow growing larger and larger on the wall. It's Aidan.

Kumal watches Aidan shoulder his rifle.

A flash of light. Kumal sees the Great Tiger collapse to the ground.

INT. GALLERY – DAY
Hearing the shot, the coolies rush into the gallery toward the ruined chapel.

INT. DEN – RUINED CHAPEL – DAY
Aidan leans over Napoleon and examines his injured arm.

> **AIDAN**
> Where did he get you?
>
> **NAPOLEAN**
> Just in the shoulder…
>
> **AIDAN**
> What's the bounty for a tiger in these parts?
>
> **NAPOLEAN**
> 150 piastres.

Aidan pulls out his handkerchief, makes a tourniquet.

AIDAN
I'll see that you get it.

Kumal is trembling in the dark. He curls up tighter, trying to hide. He hears voices nearby and can feel the mass above him start to move. Light comes in from above.

The coolies lift the carcass of the great tiger, revealing the tiger cub hiding underneath.

Exposed, Kumal decides to confront them like a real tiger. He snarls as Aidan raises his rifle. Then again, as it is lowered.

In Which McRory Runs Afoul of the Law, Kumal Joins the Circus, and L'Administrateur Stages a Tiger Hunt

Arriving at the village with his trove of statues—plus one live and one dead tiger—Aidan is greeted as a savior by the villagers and welcomed by the Chief and his beautiful daughter, Nai-Rea. The Chief claims both tigers as his reward for lending aid; before Aidan can object, the native police drive up and arrest him for looting—the Chief has been playing both sides. As his new friend is taken away, Kumal tries in vain to follow.

That night, chained to the veranda, Kumal wails miserably. Hearing him, the tigress roars in answer, and approaches the village with Sangha. Panicked villagers chase her off with torches, shots, and banging on gongs and pots; while the desperate Kumal can only watch. Now eager to be rid of this peril, the Chief sells Kumal to a traveling circus. From inside a crate lashed to the back of a truck, Kumal sees his mother give chase. She bounds onto the truck as it lurches down the road and nearly frees her cub, but is thrown off. She and Sangha watch Kumal vanish into the dust.

Meanwhile, Aidan receives a visitor in prison. The French administrator, Eugène Normandin, expresses outrage that the famed hunter has been treated so poorly—as if

it were not his idea to lock him up in the first place. He orders Aidan freed, but sees to it that he misses his ship home. The administrator has plans for him.

At the ragtag Circus Zerbino, Kumal meets the Great Zerbino himself, an all-purpose animal tamer and entertainer; Madame Zerbino; and the vicious Saladin, who sees the cub as an enemy to be vanquished. There is also the old tiger that Kumal is meant to replace, ludicrously named "Bloody Caesar." Kumal hopes for a friend, but the dispirited beast ignores him.

Normandin persuades Aidan to stage a tiger hunt for the local Prince, whose approval he needs for his scheme to build a road to bring tourists to the jungle temples. Aidan sets a trap, herding the tigress and Sangha into a deep pit where they are held in waiting. On the big day, colonists and villagers welcome the Prince and his consort, a Parisian dancer. The hunting party boards elephants while Aidan and his crew flush out the tigress. She and Sangha flee, but as the hunters close in, she hides the exhausted cub in a cave and confronts her tormen-

tors. A shot from His Excellency's rifle brings her down—but just as he is being photographed with his trophy, she leaps up and races into the forest. The bullet had only pierced her ear and stunned her.

As the furor subsides, Madame Normandin notices that her young son Raoul is missing! He has wandered off and discovered Sangha's hiding place. They are soon found, and the second brother made captive.

From inside his prison crate, Kumal sees his mother race after the truck. With a final effort she leaps aboard and tears at the rope and wood with teeth and claws—but a sudden lurch throws her off. She and Sangha comfort each other on the dusty road.

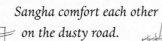

Kumal hears the boards of the crate being pried off. The cover is removed. He sees a man with an emaciated face and handlebar mustache. His hair is greasy and wavy and parted in the middle. A ringed hand comes nearer, grabs Kumal by the scruff of his neck, and shows off the pink-bellied, spitting kitten.

> ZERBINO
> And now, ladies and gentlemen, meet the man-eater!

Kumal now sees a little ragged group of humans assembled under the dirty canvas of a tent. Beyond, Kumal sees the cages of a traveling menagerie. He can make out the silhouettes of animals whose eyes are glowing in the darkness.

> ZERBINO
> If you have no objection, I think we'll call you . . . Kumal.

The mustachioed man turns the baby tiger towards him.

> ZERBINO (cont'd)
> For your information, I am Zerbino, the world-famous animal tamer and director of the Great Zerbino Circus!

Zerbino turns Kumal towards an Annamese woman dressed in a short riding skirt, who is several months pregnant.

> ZERBINO (cont'd)
> Madame Zerbino, (*He indicates the round belly of his wife*) And still cooking in the oven is my son . . .

He flashes a sharp look at her.

A burst of flame startles Kumal. A Hindu with disturbing eyes, wearing a turban and faded, baggy Turkish trousers, emerges from the shadows. He exchanges a look with Madame Zerbino as she raises her eyebrows mockingly.

> **ZERBINO**
> This fire-eating sword swallower is Saladin.

Saladin swallows a gulp of petrol, and blows out a spray, which he ignites.

> **SALADIN**
> Where did you find him? In the toy department?

> **ZERBINO**
> He's fierce enough, don't you worry.

As His Excellency poses with the tigress he has shot (but only through the ear), she suddenly leaps up, knocking him over, and flees into the forest as the other hunters fire in vain. Meanwhile, young Raoul has found Sangha's hiding place.

In Which a Tiger Skin Is Obtained by Foul Play, and Sangha Proves an Unsuitable Pet

At the circus, Kumal languishes, so miserable he refuses food. His keepers fear he will die, but the old tiger finally takes pity on him and offers his tail for a plaything. When "Bloody Caesar" has to go perform his act, he sees with satisfaction that the cub has perked up enough to eat.

At Chez Normandin, Raoul and Sangha become fast friends, playing hide-and-seek among the stuffed animal toys. At bedtime, Madame reads to them from the books of Aidan McRory, which she seems to enjoy in her own way. A favorite game is hiding from the obnoxious little dog, Bitzy, who hates Sangha; one day they are under the dining table as the adults discuss Aidan's future in the colony. Aidan wants to go upriver and see more temples with

Nai-Rea as his guide. But Normandin needs a tiger skin to present to His Excellency, who's being difficult about the road project. Meanwhile, Raoul and Sangha's antics under the table make Madame believe Aidan is playing footsie with her—until Bitzy bursts in and chases the lurkers out, laying waste to the meal.

Reluctant to hunt again, Aidan visits the circus, thinking they

might have a tiger hide he could palm off as the animal winged by the Prince. Amazed to discover Kumal there, he tries to rationalize having captured the cub, but guilt begins to gnaw at him. The scheming Saladin promises they can procure a tiger skin, but it's the old tiger he has in mind. Aidan strikes a deal, hoping his money will at least buy Kumal better food.

The hide is duly delivered to His Excellency, but the whole plot is for naught—he knows it's not "his" tiger. Returning to the circus, a horrified Aidan learns where the skin came from, and that Kumal is now doomed to replace the old tiger in the ring. As he and Nai-Rea head upriver by raft, they argue about why he should feel pity for a tiger, and whether the stone gods of the forest should be exploited or left in peace.

Weeks pass. Sangha grows. But his blissful idyll is soon to end. Bitzy still thinks he's top dog, and one day as he madly pursues Sangha through the house—wrecking Normandin's meeting with local officials—the tables turn. Cornered, Sangha lashes out in panic, and Bitzy is temporarily silenced. A hysterical Madame Normandin orders the cub banished, and over Raoul's protests they ship him off to the Prince's villa, where the old ruler had built an underground menagerie. The Prince's majordomo hopes Sangha is really as ferocious as rumored, for training beasts to fight is the purpose of this dark zoo.

ight has fallen. The facade of the stately residence, masterpiece of colonial architecture, is all in darkness. Only one light is on, in a second-floor window.

> MADAME NORMANDIN (o.s.)
> "We had to rid the village of this blood-thirsty monster and our chance came sooner than we expected."

INT. HALLWAY – RESIDENCE – NIGHT
Bitzy is furiously scratching at the closed door. From inside, we hear the voice of Madame Normandin.

> MADAME NORMANDIN (o.s.)
> "We had just set off when suddenly there was a movement in the rocks and all at once the air was filled with roaring teeth and claws."

INT. CHILD'S ROOM – RESIDENCE – NIGHT
The title of the book is *The Lion Hunt*, by Aidan McRory. Madame Normandin is reading aloud.

> MADAME NORMANDIN
> "With no time to aim, I brought the gun to my shoulder and fired. The bullet struck the man-eater full in the chest and, with a dull thud, it fell at the feet of my tracker."

Raoul and Sangha are lying in the bed, with a sheet up to their necks, their little heads on a pillow. Sangha sucks on a baby bottle which he holds in his paws out of habit.

> MADAME NORMANDIN (cont'd)
> "The beast rolled over and stared at me with its green, pellucid eyes, extending and retracting his claws in the final throes of death. We stood there, silent, before the magnificent creature. Then, according to custom, I cut open the

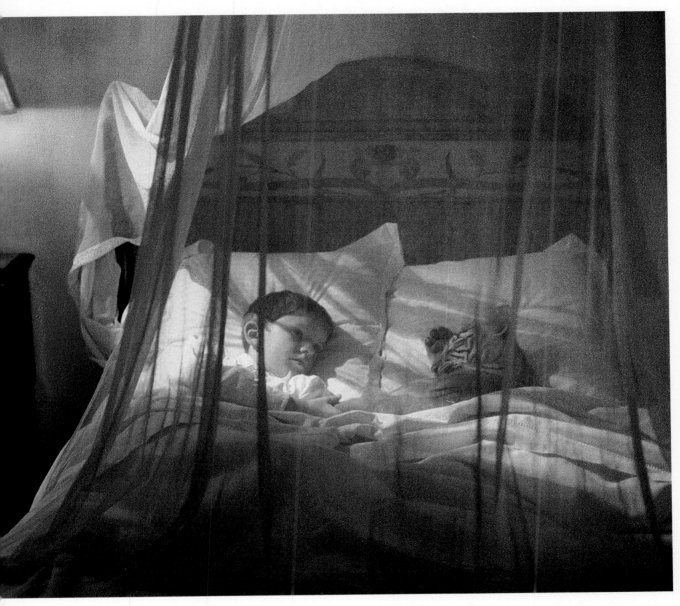

chest and gave the warm, steaming heart to my client."

In the bed, both Raoul and Sangha are nearly asleep, their eyelids growing heavy. Madame Normandin closes the book. She takes a last glance at the picture of Aidan on the cover. Under her sheer nightgown, her breathing grows more rapid. She turns out the lamp, and takes the baby bottle out of Sangha's paws. She deposits a light kiss on her son's forehead and another on Sangha's snout.

MADAME NORMANDIN
Good night, Raoul. Good night, Sangha. Pleasant dreams, my darlings.

Aidan strikes a deal for a tiger skin at the Circus Zerbino. Back at the Normandin residence, Sangha has grown into too much tiger to be a pet anymore. Though Raoul begs to keep him, he is taken away to the Prince's menagerie . . . instead of to a faraway zoo in Saigon, as his parents tell Raoul.

4

In Which Kumal and Sangha Are Bent to Human Wills, and a Contest Is Planned

Six months have passed. Kumal, now full-grown, has learned a basic repertoire of circus tricks but balks when asked to jump through a flaming hoop. Losing patience with Zerbino's slow methods, Saladin provokes Kumal, and when the tiger reacts, ties him down and beats him into submission. From then on Kumal does what he's told, but his spirit is dead.

When they next perform in the town square, the Prince's majordomo approaches Zerbino and Saladin to inquire if their tiger ("Bloody Kumal—Killer of the Mekong!") is as savage as he is billed. The Prince plans a festival, he explains—just like his father used to present, capped by a combat of wild beasts. And he has the fiercest beast around: Sangha. Zerbino hesitates, but he's sick of being upstaged by Saladin. He gets 5,000 piastres for promising that Kumal will put up a good fight.

At the palace, the Prince displays for Paulette a fabulous jewel-encrusted collar that his father had made for a fighting tiger, and which Sangha will now wear. But he speaks bitterly about the burden of living up to his father's reputation, and rails against the French who treat him like a puppet. Bewildered, Paulette watches the gorgeous bauble carried off under her nose to adorn an animal.

His Excellency decides to visit Sangha in his dungeon. It's the first time he has fully taken in the horror of this zoo—another unwelcome legacy of his powerful, primitive father—where animals are taught and equipped to be vicious. Sangha's every move emanates menace; we can only imagine what made the shy cub this way. Left alone with his tiger, the Prince confesses his feelings of inadequacy. Sangha roars and spits in answer, to which His Excellency remarks, "So you too think that one must be cruel to gain respect?"

On the day of the festival, crowds surge toward the splendidly decorated arena on the palace grounds. Among them are the Normandins, determined to get the Prince to sign papers approving the road at last—a feat that will earn the Administrator a posting back to Europe. Also on hand are Aidan and Nai-Rea, in public as a couple for the first time. Spotting Zerbino, Aidan ducks behind the arena to find the circus wagon. A listless Kumal doesn't acknowledge him, but he pleads with Zerbino and Saladin to call off the fight, knowing Kumal doesn't stand a chance. The circus hands rough him up for his pains, and he retreats, again leaving Kumal to his fate.

The limousine with golden bumpers, followed by a swarm of half-naked children, clatters over potholes.

It stops in the village square in front of the spot where the Zerbino family has set up their tent.

A turbaned chauffeur holds the back door open. The Majordomo gets out and walks over to the circus poster. We see "Bloody Kumal, the killer of the Mekong," holding the broken remains of his unfortunate tamer in his jaws.

Zerbino and Saladin come over, drawn by the shiny automobile.

MAJORDOMO
Is your tiger really ferocious?

SALADIN
Why don't you test him? If you have a spare arm or leg, here's the key to his cage.

MAJORDOMO
My master is mounting a festival. It is to be organized exactly as it was in the time of his late father. Have you heard of these ceremonies?

ZERBINO
Everyone has.

Zerbino looks suddenly concerned. He asks:

ZERBINO
What animal would he be against?

MAJORDOMO
A savage one. We have the best fighting beast I've ever known in captivity. We want an opponent that's worthy of him.

Zerbino knows that his wife's "cousin" is going to accept. This time he wants to appear as the man who makes the decisions.

ZERBINO
A special beast means a special price. Five thousand piastres.

The Majordomo hesitates, then holds out his hand to shake.

MAJORDOMO
He'd better be worth it.

SALADIN
He is. Let us know when to stop feeding him.

is Excellency, accompanied by his Majordomo, enters the labyrinth and looks about.

He arrives in front of a cage that is more spacious than the others. He stops. A young adult tiger is pacing nervously in his iron prison. Every movement has a sense of danger.

> **HIS EXCELLENCY**
> Was he born ferocious?

> **MAJORDOMO**
> He was a very shy animal when he arrived here, full of fear. It's always fear that makes us into killers.

On the tiger's neck, reflecting the fire of the torchlight, sparkles the diamond necklace.

> **HIS EXCELLENCY**
> Why do they call him Sangha?

> **MAJORDOMO**
> The Administrator's child named him.

> **HIS EXCELLENCY**
> Leave me.

At a sign from the Majordomo, a Louis Quinze chair is brought in. The Majordomo remains for a moment, hesitant.

> **MAJORDOMO**
> Your Excellency, he is very dangerous.

> **HIS EXCELLENCY**
> Leave me!

Reluctantly, the Majordomo leaves. Alone, half-smiling, the young potentate contemplates the wild animal.

Sangha stands, looking back with phosphorescent eyes.

> **HIS EXCELLENCY (cont'd)**
> Do you remember your father, Sangha? Was he a great lord of the jungle? Mine was. . . . Did all other creatures shrink in his shadow? That's how it was with

mine. . . . And was yours disappointed in his son?

The beast and the man stare at each other.

HIS EXCELLENCY (cont'd)
No. Perhaps yours was not . . .

Sangha snaps like a spring, fakes a charge and, with a savage roar, spits in His Excellency's face. He wipes his face calmly with his silk handkerchief.

He gets up and walks over to the cage. The tiger keeps his eyes on him. The young man is almost against the bars.

HIS EXCELLENCY (cont'd)
So you too think that one must be cruel in this world, do you? That one must be cruel to gain respect?

Sangha remains motionless, staring fixedly at His Excellency with luminous eyes.

5

In Which Nothing Goes as Planned, and Our Tigers Survive a Trial by Fire

At His Excellency's signal, a gong sounds to open the combat. When Sangha bursts into the arena, Raoul recognizes him at once, though he's been told Sangha went to a zoo in Saigon. Aidan stumbles back from his beating and starts to escort Nai-Rea away from this travesty. He's ready to go home and wants her to come with him.

Sangha roams the arena, seeking his opponent. Prodded by Saladin's pitchfork, Kumal enters cautiously and when he sees Sangha in battle pose, tries to retreat—but the way is barred. Sangha stalks him, charging and feinting; finally Kumal turns to face him. As they draw closer, Kumal suddenly sees a vision of his temple home and catches a familiar scent. Both tigers pause, sniff the air, then charge together in a terrifying embrace—but in an instant, combat turns to play as the brothers recognize each other. Kumal pulls Sangha along

by his tail as when they were cubs; both chase a metal ornament around like a soccer ball. Some in the crowd are amused—but not Saladin or the majordomo, who try to rouse the tigers into fight mode. For Saladin, it's a bad mistake.

In the confusion, a gate is left open and the tigers slip out, causing a panicked rush for the exits. Kumal, out of habit, jumps into his cage for refuge, but when Sangha

calls him, he leaves the cage for good. The two cut a fearful yet comic swath through the town: trampling formal gardens, invading a newsstand, scaring a bather out of the tub. Heading out into the countryside, they highjack a bus carrying livestock on its roof. Encountering the tigers on a narrow bridge, a dignitary and his chair bearers leap for the water.

But they will not be left to wreak havoc, or even to melt into the forest. Hunters gather in the village, directed by Normandin, to plan the execution of the renegade tigers. Aidan joins in for the sake of Nai-Rea and her kin. Raoul, having found and lost his tiger again, is inconsolable, though Aidan explains that such tigers, unafraid of humans and unable to hunt in the wild, will become man-eaters for real and must be killed. Soon the hunt is on, not far from the brothers' childhood home.

Fires are lit to drive Kumal and Sangha toward the guns. Turned back from one escape route after another, they are trapped—until Kumal, emboldened by his circus training, leaps through the flames to safety, then comes back and persuades Sangha to follow. Aidan, watching through binoculars, is astounded but sets off to follow them. So does Raoul, unbeknownst to his father. Boy and man both briefly reunite with the tigers they love, and Aidan holds his fire. Departing down a trail together, Kumal and Sangha call out in throaty roars. Far off, a tiger answers. "Whatever it is, maybe it can teach them to hunt," hopes Raoul. Reunited with the tigress in the final scene, the brothers lie with her peacefully by the sacred river.

Sangha pursues Kumal relentlessly around the arena. Then they rush together and fall to the ground, growling fiercely—but the fight takes a strange turn when the brothers recognize each other and start to play. Escaping through a gate left open, they send the crowd fleeing.

148

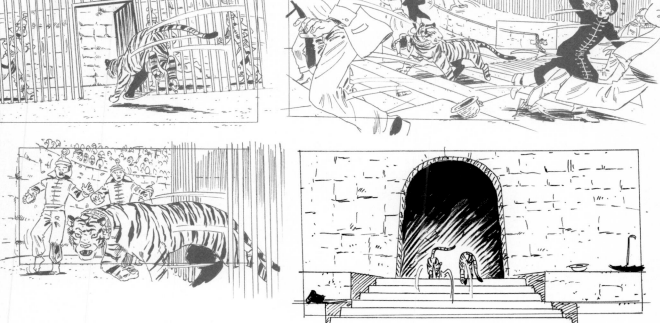

In the light of an oil lamp, Aidan and Raoul are in one corner of the veranda. They sit cross-legged, facing each other.

AIDAN
You see that old man over there, leaning on his cane, and that woman with her child? What would you say if you found out that your tiger had torn off one of their legs or killed one of them?

Nai-Rea freezes. She turns toward the sound of his voice.

RAOUL
Sangha never ate anyone.

AIDAN
No, but he will—it won't be long.

RAOUL
If he'd wanted to, he would've already done it.

At the other end of the veranda, Normandin is pacing, smoking on his pipe. He, too, is tense, listening to the exchange between Aidan and his son.

AIDAN
Raoul, he never learned to hunt. He's not afraid of people. So when he gets hungry, he'll go for the easiest prey he can find, like the women in the fields or the children. . . . You see, all great predators who escape from captivity become man-eaters when they return to the wild. They can't avoid it. It's instinct.

On the veranda, Raoul's eyes fill with tears.

RAOUL
But they're not like that . . . I know they're not.

AIDAN
No, you hope they're not. And that's only because you love Sangha.

RAOUL
And you don't love Kumal?

AIDAN
'Course I do. More than you know.

Raoul blows his nose.

RAOUL
So don't kill them. . . . Please.

In the corner near her small shrine, Nai-Rea closes her eyes. She joins her hands and starts to pray.

Outside, the jungle rustles with its mysterious life.

AIDAN (cont'd)
Raoul, I'm the one who took Kumal from the jungle. I'm also the one who let you keep Sangha. So this whole mess is my fault. And if I don't do it, somebody else will.

Kumal turns around, again facing the fire. He has already braved it once, but now he must help Sangha. Sangha watches him take a flying leap through the fiery wall. He hesitates, circles, then coils up and leaps through the flames after his brother. Watching them walk off into the forest, Aidan and Raoul hear a far-off roar, and hope for the best for the tigers they love.

TIGER CONSERVATION ORGANIZATIONS AND INFORMATION

5 TIGERS: TIGER INFORMATION CENTER *www.5tigers.org*
Excellent informational website hosted by the Minnesota Zoo, an important research and captive breeding center for tigers, and sponsored by the Save the Tiger Fund (see below). Offers tiger education, news, multimedia resources, kids' activities, teacher resources, and an extensive bibliography.

21ST CENTURY TIGER *www.21stcenturytiger.org*
Well-designed site features tiger info, news, projects, kids' page, "challenge" trips, and more. 21st Century Tiger is a conservation partnership between the Zoological Society of London and Global Tiger Patrol (see below) that funds only wild tiger conservation projects; some 40 since its launch in 1997.

CAT ACTION TREASURY (CAT) *www.felidae.org*
In cooperation with the World Conservation Union's (IUCN) Cat Specialist Group, CAT organizes and raises funds to conserve the world's 36 species of wild cats in their natural habitats. It manages the Cambodia Tiger Conservation Program, which hires former tiger hunters as community wildlife rangers. Website includes extensive links to other tiger organizations.

FLORA AND FAUNA INTERNATIONAL *www.fauna-flora.org*
Founded in 1903, FFI acts to conserve threatened species and ecosystems worldwide. One of its chief programs is in Cambodia's Cardamom Mountains, SE Asia's largest remaining natural area, where over 2 million acres of pristine forest, home to many endangered species including tigers and Asian elephants, have been protected.

GLOBAL TIGER PATROL *www.globaltigerpatrol.co.uk*
Founded in 1989, GTP works mainly in India, supporting protection, habitat conservation and restoration, people-centered conservation, research, and data collection. It provides support to Indian nongovernmental organizations that share its objectives and vital equipment and training to rangers in the field.

PROJECT TIGER *projecttiger.nic.in/index.asp*
Since 1973, Project Tiger—a program of India's Ministry of Environment and Forests—has worked to ensure a viable population of tigers in India. It has helped the Bengal subspecies to recover from the brink of extinction and currently it manages 27 tiger reserves. Extensive website features photos, tiger data, profiles of reserves, a discussion forum, and kids' section.

SAVE CHINA'S TIGERS *www.savechinastigers.net*
Interesting site devoted to the severely endangered South China subspecies, of which only 10-30 survive in the wild. Works to protect and restore ecosystems, protect wild tigers and their habitat, and find alternatives to make conservation sustainable. On the site you can vote to make the Chinese tiger the official mascot of the 2008 Beijing Olympics.

SAVE THE TIGER FUND *www.nfwf.org/programs/stf.htm*
A special project of the National Fish and Wildlife Foundation in partnership with ExxonMobil, STF is dedicated to conserving Asia's remaining wild tigers. STF and the Critical Ecosystem Partnership Fund (CEPF) have joined forces to link tiger conservation programs across Asia, a major step in unifying the efforts of many conservation organizations.

THE TIGER FOUNDATION *www.tigers.ca/index.html*
Private family foundation, inspired by a trip to China where the family's children saw a tiger paw for sale. Devoted to the preservation of wild tigers, it partners with many established groups and contributes to projects worldwide. Well-designed site contains interactive features as well as bios of leading "tiger people."

TIGRIS FOUNDATION *www.tigrisfoundation.nl*
In the southeastern tip of Russia, the last 400 Amur tigers and 40 Amur leopards roam the forests. Tigris, a Dutch organization founded in 1996, is dedicated to the survival of these endangered cats.

TRAFFIC *www.traffic.org*
This wildlife trade monitoring network is a joint program of WWF and IUCN (World Conservation Union) with offices in many countries; it works in cooperation with the Secretariat of the Convention on International Trade in Endangered Species of Wild Flora and Fauna (CITES). The tiger is one of its 10 "priority species."

WILDAID *www.wildaid.org*
WildAid works to decimate the illegal wildlife trade in our lifetimes, bring wildlife conservation to the top of the international agenda, effectively and affordably protect wilderness areas, ensure that endangered species rebound, and enable people and wildlife to survive together. Tigers are a species of special focus.

WILDLIFE CONSERVATION SOCIETY *www.wcs.org*
One of the largest and best-known international wildlife organizations, WCS saves wildlife and wild lands through careful science, international conservation, education, and the management of the world's largest system of urban wildlife parks. Conducts or supports projects in all Asian countries where tigers survive. Extensive website details its activities and provides virtual tours of its zoos.

WILDLIFE PROTECTION SOCIETY OF INDIA
www.wpsi-india.org/wpsi/index.php
Founded in 1994 by Belinda Wright, an award-winning wildlife photographer and filmmaker who took up the cause of conservation, WPSI focuses on solving India's growing wildlife crisis. It works to combat poaching and the escalating illegal wildlife trade—particularly in wild tigers.

WORLD WILDLIFE FUND
www.worldwildlife.org
WWF is a global organization acting locally through a large network of offices. Its new tiger conservation plan, *Conserving Tigers in the Wild: A WWF Framework Strategy for Action 2002-2010*, identifies seven focal landscapes where the chances of long-term tiger conservation are best and its involvement will be most valuable. Extensive online presence includes a newsroom, fact sheets and other publications, and photo gallery. *www.panda.org* (WWF International, based in Switzerland)

PATHÉ presents

The Tigers
KUMAL and SANGHA
In

TWO BROTHERS

a Film by JEAN-JACQUES ANNAUD

GUY PEARCE as Aidan McRory

JEAN-CLAUDE DREYFUS as Administrator Normandin

FREDDIE HIGHMORE Young Raoul

OANH NGUYEN His Excellency

PHILIPPINE LEROY BEAULIEU Mrs. Normandin

MOUSSA MAASKRI Saladin

VINCENT SCARITO Zerbino

MAÏ ANH LÊ Naï-Rea

JARAN PHETJAREON "SITAO" The Village Chief

STEPHANIE LAGARDE Miss Paulette

BERNARD FLAVIEN His Excellency's Majordomo

ANNOP VORAPANYA "MU" Sergeant Van Tranh

Auctioneer . . . . DAVID GANT
Verlaine . . . . TEERAWAT MULVILAI "KA-NGE"
Napoléon . . . . SOMJIN CHIMWONG "NEN"
Mrs Zerbino . . . . NOZHA KHOUADRA
Dignitary with Goldfish . . . . PRING SAKHORN
Policeman . . . . JERRY HOH
Auction room Stylish Woman . . . . JULIET HOWLAND
Auction room Companion . . . . CAROLINE WILDI
Photographer . . . . THAVIRAP TANTIWONGSE
Circus Boy . . . . BÔ GAULTIER DE KERMOAL
Fleeing Bathing Woman . . . . DELPHINE KASSEM
Assistant to Auctioneer . . . . ALAN FAIRBAIRN
Residency Butler . . . . THOMAS LARGET
Dignitaries' translator . . . . HY PEAHU
Dignitaries . . . . LUONG HAM CHAO, TRAN HONG,
CHEA IEM, NGO QUI YEN
Residency Cook . . . . MATHIAS GHIAP
Residency Servant . . . . LUONG HOAN
Circus Boy . . . . SAÏD SERRARI
Circus Boy . . . . GERARD TAN
Butcher . . . . XAVIER CASTANO
Bus Driver . . . . SUBAN PHUSO
News Stand Man . . . . CHRISTOPHE CHEYSSON

Tigers Trained and Directed by THIERRY LE PORTIER
Assisted by MONIQUE ANGEON

Written by ALAIN GODARD & JEAN-JACQUES ANNAUD

Based on an original story by JEAN-JACQUES ANNAUD

English dialogue polished by JULIAN FELLOWES

Produced by JAKE EBERTS — JEAN-JACQUES ANNAUD

Line Producer XAVIER CASTANO

Co-Producer PAUL RASSAM

U.K Co-Producer TIMOTHY BURRILL

Music by STEPHEN WARBECK

Edited by NOELLE BOISSON

Director of Photography JEAN-MARIE DREUJOU, A.F.C.

Production Designer PIERRE QUEFFELEAN

Script Supervisor and Director's Advisor
LAURENCE DUVAL-ANNAUD

Costume Designer PIERRE-YVES GAYRAUD

Visual Effects Supervisor FREDERIC MOREAU

Supervising Sound Editor EDDY JOSEPH, M.P.S.E.

Casting, USA
FRANCINE MAISLER, C.S.A.
& KATHLEEN DRISCOLL-MOHLER

Casting, U.K. JOHN and ROS HUBBARD

Casting, France SOPHIE BLANVILLAIN

Casting, Thaïland RAWEEPORN SRIMONJU JUNGMEIER "NON"

Associate Producers BEN SPECTOR, FLORE MICHIELS

First Assistant Director CHRISTOPHE CHEYSSON

Camera Operators . . . . JEAN-MARIE DREUJOU
MYRIAM VINOCOUR, ERIC BIGLIETTO
HD Digital Engineer . . . . OLIVIER GARCIA
Camera & Steadicam Operator . . . . PATRICK DE RANTER
Production Sound Mixer . . . . CHRISTIAN WANGLER
Production Supervisor . . . . JEAN-YVES ASSELIN
Production Manager . . . . PHILLIP M. KENNY
Production Manager, Thailand . . . . PAIROJ ROJLERTJANYA
Unit Manager, Asia . . . . NAOUFEL BEN YOUSSEF
Unit Manager, Thailand . . . . DAVID MITNIK
Unit Manager, France . . . . JEAN-PHILIPPE AVENEL
1st Assistant Editor . . . . STAN COLLET
2nd Unit Director . . . . XAVIER CASTANO

A French -United Kingdom Co-Production
PATHÉ RENN PRODUCTION (Paris)
TWO BROTHERS PRODUCTIONS Ltd (London)
with TF1 FILMS PRODUCTION
and the participation of CANAL +

Art Directors . . . . FRANCK SCHWARZ, STEVE SPENCE
Set Decorators . . . . . PHILIPPE TURLURE, BENOIT CISILKIEWICK
Head Greensmen . . . . . THIERRY LEMAIRE, NICOLAS CHAILLET
Special Effects Supervisor . . . . ULI NEFZER
Animatronics Supervisor . . . . PASCAL MOLINA
Second Assistant Directors . . . . BRIEUC VANDERSWALM
DANY DITTMANN
Third Assistant Directors . . . . JEAN-EMMANUEL GRAINE
MARJORIE TAPPERT
Storyboard Artist . . . . FANNY VASSOU
Business Affairs Manager . . . . LEONARD GLOWINSKI
Financial Controller . . . . MYRIAM KAUFMANN
Legal Counsel . . . . SYLVIE COEN
Financial Supervisor . . . . NICOLE HEITZMANN
Production Accountants . . . . SARAH MILLAR,
FRANÇOISE BOUILLON-POMMEROLLE,
CORINNE SAGLIO, EDITH PAVAGEAU
Assistant Production Accountant . . . . EMILE PLOIX
Production Coordinators . . . . DANIELLE DUMANOIR
MARION ABADIE

Assistant to Mr. Jake Eberts	IRENE LYONS
Assistant to Mr. Timothy Burrill	JACQUELINE EDWARDS
Stills Photographer	DAVID KOSKAS
Focus Pullers	JEAN-PAUL VALLORANI NICOLAS RIDEAU, CENDRINE DEDISE
HD Digital Assistant Operator	SEBASTIEN NAAR
Film Loaders	VINCENT TRIVIDIC, ARNAUD DELANNOY, BERTRAND ETIENNE
Continuity	BETTY GREFFET
Sound Maintenance	PETER MURPHY
Dialogue Coach	CELIA BANNERMAN
Extras Casting, France	CHRISTINE CAMPION
Unit Production Coordinator	SANDRA CASTANO
Unit Managers	OLIVIER HELIE, MAXIME BOCHNER
Location Managers	PERRINE COULOGNER, PHILIPPE MOTTIN, JEAN GUIRAUD, EMMANUEL RIGAUT
Transportation Captain, Cambodia	CHRISTINE JANEAU
Unit Manager for Animals, Asia	YVES HERSEN
Animal Trainers	HUBERT WELLS, RANDY MILLER
Assistant Animal Trainers	KAREEN LE PORTIER, JACQUES DA SILVA MARTINS, DAVID FAIVRE, DAVID WEISER, ALINE RIBET, MARIE-EMMANUELLE ROSE, CHARLIE WEISER
Small Animal Trainers	GUY DEMAZURE, ANNE DEMAZURE
Veterinarian	ALEXIS LÉCU
Dog Trainer	PATRICK PITTAVINO
Assistant Costume Designer	CATHERINE BOISGONTIER
Workshop Costumers	ANNE VERSEL, URSULA PAREDES CHOTO, VERA BOUSSICOT, TESS HAMMAMI
Props & Jewelry Master	LORENZO MANCIANTI
Wardrobe Masters/Dressers	GRAHAM HUNTER, BRIGITTE LALEOUSE, NATHALIE CAUSSE
Wardrobe	ANNICK ALATERRE-REDON, GAEL ROGER, OLIVIER ROCHETTE
Military Costume Advisor	SERGE ANTOINE LEGRAND
Make-Up & Hair Designer	SUZANNE JANSEN
Make-Up Designer	FRANÇOISE CHAPUIS-ASSELIN
Hair Designer	AGATHE DUPUIS
Make-Up/Hair Artists	GEMMA WAUGH, LISA PICKERING
Assistant Art Director	EMMANUELLE PUCCI
Art Department Coordinator	JEAN JACQUES BOULBEN
Prop Buyers	EMMANUEL DELIS, GILLES ISCAN, JEAN-CHRISTOPHE MINFRAY
Model Maker	NADEGE ARCHAMBAUD
Dressing Props	PHILIPPE MARGOTTIN, CYRILLE AUTISSIER
Standby Propmen	MICHEL CONCHE, BERNARD DUCROCQ
Head Drapesman	JACQUES KAZANDJIAN
Drapesman	FRANCINE CROSBOIS
Armourer	DANIEL BAUER (MARATIER)
Construction Manager	GILLES LABOULANDINE
Head Carpenter	OLIVIER FOUCHER
Head Construction Grips	HERVE LAGILLE, CHRISTOPHE LUNAY
Head Painter	JEAN-FRANÇOIS JUVANON
Scenic Painter	GILBERT PIGNOL
Key Sculptor	FRANÇOIS-PIERRE DEBERRE
Sculptor	ARNAUD BEAUTÉ
Animatronics Art Director	DENIS GASTOU
Animatronics First Assistant	VIRGINIE MOLINA
Animatronics Mechanic Coordinator	PERRINE POIRIER
Special Effects Technicians	TILL HERTRICH, MICHAEL LUPPINO, WOLFGANG HIGLER, THOMAS THIELE

Gaffer	JEAN-CLAUDE REUX
Electricians	PATRICK GASCHÉ, ARNAUD HERMELINE
Genny Operator	TAHAR BOUALAM
Key Grip	PAUL-CLAUDE BESSIERE
Grips	JOEL TOUPENSE, ERIC BONNAIRE, DOMINIQUE GONNIN, BRUNO ROZA
Motion Control Operator	ALEX DE HEUS
Motion Control & Steadicam Operator	ROB VAN GELDER
Nurse	MICHELLE DELAPORTE-CASTANO
International Public Relations	MELANIE HODAL, MHPR
Unit Publicist	AMANDA J. BRAND
Making-Of Director and Camera	DOMINIQUE CHEMINAL
Post-Production Supervisor	MICHAEL SAXTON
Post-Production Coordinator	VERITY WISLOCKI
Assistant Editors	VIRGINIE SEGUIN, LIONEL CASSAN
Sound Effects Editors	JAMES HARRISON, MARTIN CANTWELL, A.M.P.S.
Dialogue/ADR Editor	COLIN RITCHIE, M.P.S.E.
Assistant Sound Editors	RICHARD FORDHAM, SIMON CHASE
Re-Recording Mixers	MIKE PRESTWOOD SMITH, MATTHEW GOUGH

VISUAL EFFECTS BY ÉCLAIR NUMERIQUE

Artistic Supervision	PHILIPPE SOEIRO
On Stage Supervision	CHRISTIAN RAJAUD
Coordination	SARAH FLAMENT
Digital Artists	MARC LATIL, PIERRE BLAIN, PHILIPPE BLEIN, THIERRY FLAMENT, JEREMY JUSTICE, FRANCIS LENOIR, OLIVIER DEBERT, CLAIRE CUNIER, AUDE NGUYEN, MELODIE STEVENS, BENJAMIN RIBIERE

CREOCOLLECTIVE

Supervision	JEAN-MARC DEMMER
Production	BAPTISTE ANDRIEUX, JULIE PINSON
Digital Artists	HARRY BARDAK, RICHARD RAIMBAULT, SEAN FEENE, BREK TAYLOR
Animation Supervisor	ROMUALD CAUDROIT

VISUAL FACTORY

Supervision	IGOR SEKULIC
Production	GIULIANO D. VIGANO, CHRIS HARWOOD
Digital Artists	RAJAT ROY, MARTA GONZALEZ, DAVID SCOTT, NATHALIE McDONALD

DIGITAL LABORATORY: LABORATORIES ÉCLAIR PARIS

Production Supervisor	OLIVIER CHIAVASSA
Technical Coordinators	CHRISTIAN NINAUD PHILIPPE REINAUDO
Post-Production Coordinators	CATHERINE ATHON PHILIPPE TOURRET
Digital Grading	YVAN LUCAS, BRUNO PATIN
ADR Mixer	PAUL CARR
Foley Artists	FELICITY COTTRELL, RUTH SULLIVAN
Foley Mixer	ED COLYER
Voice Casting	BRENDAN DONNISON, M.P.S.E., VANESSA BAKER
ADR Recording	GOLDCREST POST PRODUCTION
Titles Designed by	RICHARD MORRISON, FIG PRODUCTIONS
Titles Post-Production	ONE POST
Sound Re-Recorded at	DE LANE LEA
Music Editors	DINA EATON, PETER CLARKE
Music Supervisors	BECKY BENTHAM, NYREE PINDER for HOTHOUSE MUSIC Ltd